Birds of the Tropical Andes

Birds of the Tropical Andes

Photography by
OWEN DEUTSCH

Text by
MICHAEL J. PARR
President, American Bird Conservancy

Contributors:
**CONSTANTINO AUCCA CHUTAS,
SARA INÉS LARA, MARTIN SCHAEFER,**
and **RODRIGO W. SORIA AUZA**

With a foreword by
ALVARO JARAMILLO

 American Bird Conservancy

Princeton University Press
Princeton and Oxford

DEDICATION

This book is dedicated to ADRIAN FORSYTH and ENRIQUE ORTIZ, whose belief in American Bird Conservancy resulted in our first large grants for the conservation of bird habitat in the tropical Andes. Everything else grew from this. Thank you both so much.

Copyright © 2025 American Bird Conservancy and Owen Deutsch
Foreword copyright © 2025 by Alvaro Jaramillo
Copyright © 2025 by Constantino Aucca Chutas
Copyright © 2025 by Sara Inés Lara
Copyright © 2025 by Martin Schaefer
Copyright © 2025 by Rodrigo W. Soria Auza

Princeton University Press is committed to the protection of copyright and the intellectual property our authors entrust to us. Copyright promotes the progress and integrity of knowledge created by humans. By engaging with an authorized copy of this work, you are supporting creators and the global exchange of ideas. As this work is protected by copyright, any reproduction or distribution of it in any form for any purpose requires permission; permission requests should be sent to permissions@press.princeton.edu. Ingestion of any PUP IP for any AI purposes is strictly prohibited.

Published by Princeton University Press
41 William Street, Princeton, New Jersey 08540
99 Banbury Road, Oxford OX2 6JX
press.princeton.edu

GPSR Authorized Representative: Easy Access System Europe - Mustamäe tee 50, 10621 Tallinn, Estonia, gpsr.requests@easproject.com

All Rights Reserved

ISBN 978-0-691-26068-6
ISBN (e-book) 978-0-691-26095-2

Library of Congress Control Number: 2025932926

British Library Cataloging-in-Publication Data is available

Editorial: Robert Kirk and Megan Mendonça
Production Editorial: Karen Carter
Text Design: D & N Publishing, Wiltshire, UK
Jacket/Cover Design: Wanda España
Production: Steven Sears
Publicity: William Pagdatoon and Caitlyn Robson-Iszatt
Copyeditor: Charles J. Hagner
Front cover credit: James's Flamingos (*Phoenicoparrus jamesi*) by Owen Deutsch

Publication of this book has been aided by Owen Deutsch

Royalties support American Bird Conservancy

This book has been composed in Inria Serif (body) and Futura PT (headings)

Printed in Italy

10 9 8 7 6 5 4 3 2 1

CONTENTS

Foreword by Alvaro Jaramillo … 6
Preface … 7
About this Book … 8
Introduction … 12
   American Bird Conservancy in the Andes … 14
   Glossary for Captions … 15

1 THE PACIFIC SLOPE AND WESTERN ANDES … 16
THE CHOCÓ … 18
Biogeography and History … 20
Bird Diversity and Specialties … 22
Conservation … 23
Birding and Photography Sites … 25
From the Field: Ecuador … 48

TUMBESIA AND THE MARAÑÓN VALLEY … 50
Biogeography and History … 52
Bird Diversity and Specialties … 54
Conservation … 57
Birding and Photography Sites … 58

THE LAND OF THE NAZCA … 66
Biogeography and History … 68
Bird Diversity and Specialties … 71
Conservation … 73
Birding and Photography Sites … 74

2 THE COLOMBIAN ANDES … 94
Biogeography and History … 96
Bird Diversity and Specialties … 97
Conservation … 98
Birding and Photography Sites … 99
From the Field: Colombia … 130

3 THE HIGH ANDES … 132
THE PÁRAMO … 134
Biogeography and History … 137
Bird Diversity and Specialties … 138
Conservation … 139
Birding and Photography Sites … 141

POLYLEPIS FOREST … 144
Biogeography and History … 146
Bird Diversity and Specialties … 148
Conservation … 149
Birding and Photography Sites … 151
From the Field: Peru … 154

THE ALTIPLANO AND PUNA … 156
Biogeography and History … 158
Bird Diversity and Specialties … 161
Conservation … 162
Birding and Photography Sites … 165

4 THE EAST SLOPE … 178
CLOUD FOREST … 180
Biogeography and History … 182
Bird Diversity and Specialties … 185
Conservation … 186
Birding and Photography Sites … 189

AMAZONIA … 212
Biogeography and History … 214
Bird Diversity and Specialties … 216
Conservation … 218
Birding and Photography Sites … 221

THE SOUTHEASTERN DRY FOOTHILLS … 240
Biogeography and History … 242
Bird Diversity and Specialties … 244
Conservation … 245
Birding and Photography Sites … 247
From the Field: Bolivia … 256

Migration to and from the Tropical Andes … 258
Photographer's Statement … 260
About the Photographer and Author … 261
Further Reading … 262
Index … 262

FOREWORD

I FIRST LEARNED of Mike Parr from his book *Parrots: A Guide to Parrots of the World*, coauthored with Tony Juniper. I had also worked on a book in that series and immediately felt kinship. I always enjoyed Mike's book, so it was wonderful to eventually become more aware of his work with American Bird Conservancy, meet at various functions, and even get to watch birds together here and there. Mike is one of those rare individuals who not only are on the forefront of conservation, doing work that is imperative to the future health of our planet, but also are keen, dyed-in-the-wool birdwatchers. I appreciate knowing folks like Mike, who are at once world-class in their field yet are excited to grab some coffee, wake up early, and see the local birds wherever they are on that day, people of knowledge and passion. Similarly, Owen Deutsch is a renowned photographer who has specialized in beauty, first for many years as a fashion photographer and since 2002 as a photographer dedicated to showing people the beauty of birds—and through that, providing a better understanding of the conservation challenges these avian beauties are facing.

I am also one of those birders who have taken a passion for birds and turned it into a career serving birds, science, birders, and conservation. As such, it was with great excitement that I learned of this book by Mike and Owen, *Birds of the Tropical Andes*. This is the most biodiverse region on Earth, with some of the most spectacular birds and stunning habitats found anywhere. The tropical Andes are like a dreamland for a naturalist, a region of the world where you can move up the mountain and see new creatures, different from those where you started, and the higher you go, the more different they are. Then you can drop down the other side of the Andes, and the same pattern recurs but with a new and different set of birds and animals. The Andes are the most impressive set of mountains for the birder and naturalist, and yes, they are compared to other important mountains, such as the Himalayas—yet none are quite like the Andes. The Andes are extremely long; they form a backbone to the continent of South America, and they not only are the spine but also act like a permeable wall. They divide one side from the other, shifting the regime of rain; they create wet areas on the windward side and dry rain shadows on the leeward side. They divide different forests and have done so for enough time that speciation has occurred, creating different avifaunas on each side of the peaks. You add to this the fortunate situation of having a cold-water ocean current to the west, the Humboldt Current, and this gives life to the regimes of dry and wet climates in a way that is much more complex than in other mountain chains. The Colombian Andes take this to yet another level, dividing into three ranges, each with a major river valley between them, and each range having a different climate on its east and west flank. This is like a supercharger to speciation and biodiversity generation. Nowhere else on Earth is quite like this part of the tropical Andes. It is no accident that Colombia has more bird species than any other place on Earth. This amazing fork in the Andes creates this awesome, incredible, wonderful part of the world. This is Mecca to anyone interested in natural history.

How can one not be excited about the birds of the tropical Andes? They are irresistible. Owen's photos reveal the incredible set of gorgeous, feathered creatures that live here. The photos alone are enough to thrill and excite. The book itself might attract with the photos, but in the text, we really understand what makes this piece of Earth so important and vital. Mike summarizes what makes each section of the tropical Andes, from coast to mountaintops, special from a climate and habitat perspective, and also the First Nation's history on these lands. As you would expect from one of the principals in New World bird conservation, Mike comments extensively on reserves set up for people to visit and help conserve specific sites, as well as the overall conservation situation for the ecosystems detailed in the book. The notes on which birds are the specialties in each region, and where to go to see them, are superb.

I think you will find that your first response to the book will be to want to hop on a plane and visit some of these areas, and you should. Conservation works when people take an interest and local communities see that this interest means that the trees and birds are more valuable existing as they do, instead of being subjected to any one of the activities that can destroy them while earning only short-term profits. This book is such a joyous exploration of the Andes and what makes them special. I thank Mike and Owen for taking us on this important trip—which makes me, like you, want to hop on a plane and return to these magical lands.

ALVARO JARAMILLO

PREFACE

IN MY WORK as president of American Bird Conservancy, I have been fortunate to visit the tropical Andes almost annually for the past couple of decades. I grew up in England, a country with about two hundred regular breeding bird species. I used to have a friend whose bedroom wall had a large poster showing a number of galaxies. It had a little note saying, "You are here," and another one with an arrow pointing to some distant location across the Milky Way that said, "All the good stuff is here." That was how it felt as a birder, knowing that most of the world's birds were somewhere else. South America always seemed like such a far-off place to me, and the birds were intimidating, with so many similar species of tyrannulets, antbirds, and funariids.

As a child, I collected dilapidated Victorian displays of South American birds, many of which were hummingbirds. These had been popular in the late nineteenth century, but inevitably, the glass domes under which they were preserved eventually cracked, leaving the emeralds, sylphs, coronets, and sunangels to gather dust over the next century or so in various old homes and junk shops. Enter eight-year-old me, and their future was decided. I bought all that I could. I think my parents secretly disposed of them one day when I wasn't paying attention, because eventually they just vanished—but I loved them dearly while I had them. I was never able to identify that many of the birds, but I know at least that I had a beautiful glossy Pompadour Cotinga. Even as a preteen, I could tell what that was, since it was also in my *Birds of the World* book (the large-format Austin and Singer publication).

By the time I was a teenage birder, a trip to the Andes still seemed very daunting and not very realistic. I let my fears of identification failure and my lack of Spanish lead me first to Asia, but South America and the Andes always called from the background, "We're here! When are you coming?" After I got my hands on a copy of Delacour and Amadon's monograph *Curassows and Related Birds* and saw the illustrations of Nocturnal Curassow and White-winged Guan, I made up my mind that I had to brace for the flycatchers and furnariids and find some way to get to the tropical Andes.

High-wire specialist Karl Wallenda once said, "Being on the tightrope is living; everything else is waiting." That sentiment holds with me for birding in the Andes. Field time in the Andes for me is like nothing else. It is my perfect thing; I can't be much happier than that. Adding my family and strawberry ice cream—OK, that would be even better—but the baseline would still be the same. Out in the cloud forest with my camera, or crouching on a trail looking for a tapaculo—even being stung by hornets as I searched for Giant Antpitta. Don't care. It's the most fun I can have with birds.

Back in 1997, I was on a trip to Mindo, Ecuador. It was about 4:30 a.m., and I was standing, shivering and wet, next to my friend Vinicio Perez (who now runs the famous Birdwatcher's House, near Mindo). The Toyota truck had just made it across the two-plank bridge only then to get stuck in deep, muddy ruts. I had stepped onto a narrow, wet, grassy verge to avoid the slipping, swerving truck, only to realize that the grass ended at the edge of my shoes. Shining my powerful flashlight into the void, I noticed that it didn't reach bottom. I had been standing on the slippery edge of a cliff several hundred feet high. After we got some vegetation under the tires to gain traction, we set off again to reach the trailhead.

After we forded a torrential river arm in arm, I slung a video camera, protected in a plastic trash bag, over my shoulder, and Vinicio turned to me and whispered, "Mike, now the going gets tough." I was to climb a one-hundred-foot mudslide using the few tree roots that stuck out along its edges for handholds, then shimmy up onto a steep, sloping, two-square-foot section of tree trunk in the pitch dark. There I was to hide under a sack and remain motionless until it became light. If I could pull this off, I would be sitting in the direct center of a large Andean Cock-of-the-rock lek.

The magical hour or two that followed—surrounded by a dozen or so frenzied, crowing, bright scarlet males—left a lasting impression. It is experiences like these that I often return to when thinking of my greatest moments in birding—and in life as a whole. I would not miss these for anything, and I hope that this book will be an inspiration to you to grab a field guide (or download an app), a pair of binoculars, and your passport—and book your trip to the Andes to experience the greatest birding show on the planet. This is something that my friend and fellow photographer Owen Deutsch and I have done together now on several occasions. Owen's pictures are definitely the next best thing to seeing these amazing birds for yourself, and I hope you thoroughly enjoy this volume. As you think about the birds themselves and the prospect of seeing them firsthand, please also consider that they are fragile and won't be around forever unless we take care to conserve them. With that in mind, please also consider joining American Bird Conservancy (www.abcbirds.org). Your support will help to pay for work that is creating and sustaining protected areas for many of the amazing species covered in this book.

Thank you.

MICHAEL J. PARR
President, American Bird Conservancy

ABOUT THIS BOOK

BIRDS OF THE TROPICAL ANDES was conceived by bird photographer and conservationist Owen Deutsch and me during a bird photography trip to Ecuador in January of 2023. It is the second volume that we have collaborated on, the first being *Bringing Back the Birds*, published by Braided River in 2019. Both of us have spent considerable time in the Andes independently, and we have also carried out four joint photographic expeditions to the region, including travels in Ecuador, Peru, and Bolivia.

This book is intended to convey the stunning diversity and unique beauty of Andean birds. The Andes can be regarded as one of the key epicenters of bird diversification on our planet, with many unusual endemic species (birds found nowhere else). The region also has many highly threatened species, and the work of American Bird Conservancy and its partners that are based in the Andes is designed to ensure that none of these species ever becomes extinct. We hope that by exploring and reading through this volume, you will be inspired both to visit the Andean region to experience its birds and unique culture for yourself, and to consider providing support for American Bird Conservancy (see www.abcbirds.org) to help continue and expand its work in the region.

The book is organized into biogeographic chapters that perform a virtual transect across the Andes from west to east—starting in the Pacific Ocean, beneath which the Nazca tectonic plate has been moving east below the South American Plate to drive the Andean mountains skyward for the past thirty-five million years or so. Each chapter contains sections on the biogeography and cultural history, the bird highlights of each life zone, conservation issues, and birding and photographic opportunities for visitors. From the Pacific, the narrative continues upslope across the western foothills, recognizing the variety of habitats and topography that are found from Colombia in the north to the altiplano of Bolivia in the south. Since the moisture gradient and landforms vary across the region, the book is divided into subsections relating to the unique characteristics of, for example, the multiple cordilleras of the Colombian Andes, the wet Chocó region, and the dry northern reaches of the Atacama Desert and its environs. The reader's journey continues east across the high plateaus and lakes of the Andes and then plunges some ten to fifteen thousand feet downslope to the eastern foothills and the western edge of Amazonia. The Amazon River depends on the Andes for most of its water, and while not considered part of the Andes topographically, it is inexorably tied to the mountains biogeographically. By necessity, we have focused only on the most major unique ecological zones in the Andean region, and so the coverage is not fully complete. Depending on classification, an almost infinite number of habitats and microhabitats are potentially represented in the Andean nations, and some of these, such as mangroves and mudflats, are not restricted to this geography. This book should therefore be considered an entry point into this amazing world of Andean bird and biological diversity, not an endpoint.

Each region covered is lavishly illustrated with stunning photographs of some of the birds that can be found there, and the chapter text and photographic captions provide greater detail and background on the birds and their habitats. Each chapter covers a different region and is organized to provide information that may not be found in traditional field or travel guides and will be of use to readers interested in visiting the Andes. We also include essays written by leading conservationists in the region, providing their personal perspectives on birds, habitats, and conservation needs in the Andes. This is not intended to be a scientific reference book per se, but instead an inspirational book that encourages participation in bird tourism and conservation. We therefore do not use citations throughout the text, but at the back of the book, we do provide suggestions for further relevant reading. Please note that, where possible, we have provided full habitat names (capitalized) as referenced in Campbell, Behrens, Hesse, and Chaon's *Habitats of the World*, published in 2021 by Princeton University Press. By referring to this volume, you will be able to obtain additional details on the biogeography and ecology of each of these specific habitat types. Note that both common and scientific names of birds are those used by eBird.

PHOTO OVERLEAF: **RED-FRONTED MACAWS** (*Ara rubrogenys*) gather in trees surrounding a clearing at the Red-fronted Macaw Reserve, which lies along the Mizque River in southeastern Bolivia. These spectacular, Critically Endangered parrots are benefiting from protection from poaching there thanks to the work of Asociación Armonía and local communities. COUNTRY ENDEMIC (BOLIVIA). CR

No book of this magnitude can be completed without a team of people, and we are extremely grateful to our many friends and collaborators who have made this book possible. In particular, we would like to thank our publisher, Robert Kirk of Princeton University Press; our colleagues and main field team participants, Constantino Aucca Chutas, Juan Carlos Crespo, Nathan Goldberg, Silverio Duri, Jose Balderrama, and Rodrigo Soria Auza; and our colleagues at home base who helped with the many suggestions and the photo optimization required for the project—in particular, Claire Gillman, Natalie Garcia, Taylor Nettnin, and Clare Nielsen. Special thanks are also due to Rona Talcott for her guidance in the early stages of the project and her constant support and encouragement throughout the endeavor. We also really appreciate the manuscript reviews and feedback from Iain Campbell, Constantino Aucca Chutas, Daniel Lebbin, and Martin Schaefer; bird identification and text and photo caption reviews by Nathan Goldberg; and the written contributions from our partners in the Andean region, Constantino Aucca Chutas, Sara Inés Lara, Martin Schaefer, and Rodrigo Soria Auza. Sincere thanks, too, to Alvaro Jaramillo for providing the beautifully written foreword. Also to layout artist Shane O'Dwyer, and proof-reader Stephanie Sakson.

Adding to the bibliography at the end of the book, we would particularly like to thank and cite eBird, BirdLife International and the BirdLife Data Zone (which, for example, provides data on Endemic Bird Areas), Lynx Edicions and particularly its *Illustrated Checklist of the Birds of the World*, and the several excellent national field guides to the region (including field guide apps for several countries), as well as the classic (and epic) *Birds of the High Andes* by Jon Fjeldså and Niels Krabbe. eBird provides a number of useful tools to gather and disseminate information on the birds of the Andes, including birding hotspots, individual species ranges, and species bar charts for particular locations. The BirdsEye app also provides a great way to access and study eBird data using a different and, for some tasks, easier-to-use interface. While Xeno-Canto is also worthy of mention as another great resource for Andean bird songs and calls, we did not use it as a research tool for this volume in particular.

BUFF-TAILED CORONET (*Boissonneaua flavescens*) is found in mid-elevation forests from around 5,000 to 8,000 feet in altitude. It is relatively common in the right habitat, and ranges from Venezuela to Ecuador. The species can appear almost luminous in the right light, and is common at feeders such as at the Las Tángaras reserve in Colombia, and at Birdwatcher's House near Mindo, Ecuador.

INTRODUCTION

THE ANDES ARE the world's longest mountain chain and include Mount Chimborazo (Ecuador), whose peak, at 20,548 feet above sea level, is actually slightly farther from the center of Earth than the peak of Mount Everest due to the "equatorial bulge" caused by Earth's rotation. (This makes Earth an oblate spheroid, rather than a perfect sphere.) On average, though, the Andes are not as high as the Himalayas (Earth's highest mountain range), and unlike the Himalayas, they are also highly volcanic, with about 150 currently active volcanoes across their 4,300-mile extent. Despite being slightly lower than the Himalayas overall, the Andes still have about seventy-five peaks of 20,000 feet or more in elevation and exhibit a more complex overall topography.

The Andes are also a bird paradise. Of the seven countries that have the most recorded bird species on Earth, no fewer than five (including the top two, Colombia and Peru) include parts of the Andes mountain chain in their national territory. The two most important continental Endemic Bird Areas on Earth also lie in the western Andes. So why are the Andes so good for bird diversity? First, Earth's tropics tend to have greater species richness than temperate areas. This is because the tropics benefit from twelve months of consistent sunlight, allowing a year-round growing season for plants. Flowers bloom continuously and, for example, support a staggering diversity of hummingbird species along with honeycreepers and flowerpiercers. Fruits—such as figs—are also consistently available, providing nourishment for birds like parrots, toucans, and cotingas. The relatively warmer temperatures and abundant plants of the tropics also allow insects, small mammals, and cold-blooded vertebrates to remain active year-round. These insects, small lizards, and rodents then provide a stable, reliable food source for birds.

Moisture also plays a key role in creating conditions for lush vegetation—and hence for most other biodiversity—to thrive. In the western Andes, this moisture comes primarily from the tropical Pacific Ocean, with wetter and drier periods governed by prevailing winds and pressure systems that shift seasonally. In some areas, such as the Colombian and Ecuadorian Chocó region, this moisture is delivered as heavy—often torrential—rain that has created and still supports a vibrant (though highly threatened) lowland rain forest. In others, such as the central Peruvian coast, dense seasonal fog banks support a lush, low-lying carpet of greenery (most often found in isolated sites known as *lomas*) characterized by heliotropes, *Verbena*, and cacti. Yet other areas, such as some inter-Andean valleys, the high plains of the puna, and the Pacific foothills of Tumbesia, are relatively starved of rain, and this creates another set of unique ecological niches. It is this ecological richness and habitat diversity—from altitudes close to sea level in the arid scrub and thorn forest of the Pacific foothills to above the tree line on slopes covered with sparse, low-lying, hardy grasses, cacti, and cushion plants in the high mountains—that really drive bird speciation and niche adaptation. And it is in the Andes that this diversity reaches its global crescendo.

So the tropics provide an ideal environment for birds to thrive, and there is a vast array of Andean ecosystems, but why are there so many bird species in the Andes specifically, compared with other regions of the planet? Well, Earth's highest mountain range, the Himalayas, does have high biodiversity, but the Himalayas lie north of the tropics, are less than half the length of the Andes, and have an east-west orientation, hence spanning a narrower latitudinal range. Africa has significant landmass in the tropics but has relatively fewer variations in topography, compared with South America. In Asia, there is less landmass in the tropics, and much of this is comprised of islands. Islands, of course, can also be engines of speciation and varied biodiversity due to their isolation, and, indeed, Indonesia ranks fourth globally in terms of bird species richness by country, but it is still more than a hundred species behind Colombia, which is the current (though sometimes disputed by Peru!) global leader at 1,958 bird species. The Andes are the clear winner.

Another important yet more sobering bird statistic is that three of the world's countries with the most globally threatened birds are also found in the Andean region. It is not surprising that countries with more bird species also have more threatened birds, but there are specific reasons that the Andes have a concentration of such species. When deciding which species are threatened with extinction, BirdLife International scientists examine a range of factors, including the range extent and population size of each species and the extent of the threats it faces. One factor in the Andes that makes species more prone to inclusion on the threatened list is that many birds there have extremely specialized and limited ecological niches and have become isolated in remote valleys or close to high peaks. This propensity leads birds toward smaller range and population sizes—and sometimes these alone are enough to qualify a species for consideration as being threatened. For such species, a sudden shift in status, such as a rapid decline caused by habitat loss or climate change, could be sufficient to further upgrade their threat status.

Another major factor contributing to species status is the degree of threat each species faces. While the tropical Andes may seem like a remote wilderness to some, significant parts of the region have in fact been densely settled for centuries. For most people, the history of the Andes is synonymous with that of the Incan Empire. However, Inca rule reached its peak in the

INTRODUCTION

1500s—rather recent in comparison to the earlier Chavín, Paracas, Nazca, and Huari civilizations, which predated the Inca by more than a millennium. By the time the Incan Empire was at its height, more than twelve million people already occupied the Andes, in a region spanning from northern Ecuador to central Chile. Llamas were domesticated long before the days of the Incas, and the farming of corn and other crops was also widespread well before the European colonization, which began to pick up in the sixteenth century. The Spanish conquest of the Incas initially began in 1532, and this marked a dramatic watershed in the environmental history of the region. While Peru (mostly unknowingly) contributed the potato to the rest of the world, Spain brought cattle to the Andes. As the human population began to grow, land clearance for small pastures spread across the region. Today, the region's human population is about seventy-five million, and land use practices are much less sustainable than they were in the days of the Incas. The primary threat driving bird habitat loss has been land clearance for agriculture and (especially) for cattle farming by members of small rural communities working to support their families. It is projected that the region's human population will begin to decline in the next fifty years, and rural populations have already begun to move to the large cities, but historic deforestation has already devastated large areas that were once pristine habitats. People need to survive and thrive in these communities, although this threat to forested areas has substantially reduced the amount of habitat available to bird species with tiny global ranges and specialized ecological needs.

Given the degree of endemicity and the scale of threats in the Andean region, it is perhaps surprising that, to date, the region has experienced only a single definite bird extinction—that of the Colombian Grebe, which disappeared from Lake Tota in Colombia sometime in the mid- to late 1970s. While it is tragic to lose even one species, this is good news for the region's birds overall, but the situation still remains perilous for a number of additional species that are of serious conservation concern, including some that have not been seen in recent times (such as the Sinú Parakeet and Turquoise-throated Puffleg). These species of concern include thirty-nine Endangered and Critically Endangered birds in Colombia, twenty-five in Ecuador, twenty-eight in Peru, twelve in Bolivia, and twenty in Venezuela (several of these are found outside the Andean region, however). While this is far from an ideal situation for bird conservationists, there is real hope that further species extinctions can be averted. In recent decades, a significant effort to stave off species losses has begun to take shape, led by both governmental and nongovernmental organizations based in the region. One factor that has played a role in helping to advance bird conservation in the Andes is that a significant number of North American-breeding migrants winter there. International efforts to conserve these species have picked up since the 1980s, when declines in migratory neotropical birds first started to be noticed in a major way (for example, as documented in John Terborgh's 1989 book *Where Have All the Birds Gone?*). Species that winter in the Andes in significant numbers and are familiar to North American bird lovers include Blackburnian, Canada, and Cerulean Warblers; Swainson's Thrush; Summer Tanager; Broad-winged Hawk; and Olive-sided and Acadian Flycatchers, among others. "Decline of the North American Avifauna," a paper published in the journal *Science* in 2019, showed that bird declines were far more extensive than scientists had previously understood. In fact, approximately three billion birds had been lost from the North American breeding population since 1970. These data sent shock waves around the conservation community, and it is likely that they will encourage greater investment in conservation over time.

Several groups of birds are unique to, or characteristic of, the Andes. These include several grebe species found only on high-altitude Andean lakes, including the Junin and Titicaca Grebes—and these species sometimes share these lakes with the unique Giant Coot and Andean Avocet; Andean and James's Flamingos, which nest primarily on shallow lagoons in the high Andes of Bolivia, Chile, and Argentina; the Torrent Duck, an agile species capable of negotiating some of the fastest of all rapids; caracaras, Black-chested Buzzard-Eagles, and majestic Andean Condors that soar across the high Andean plains and valleys; elusive guans and duetting wood-quail that hide below the cloud forest understory; seedsnipe, including the large Rufous-bellied Seedsnipe, which seems like the Andes' answer to a ptarmigan; a huge diversity of hummingbirds, ranging from the spectacular Marvelous Spatuletail to the impressive Giant Hummingbird (which is in the process of being split into two species, one of which has a spectacular migration); Toucan Barbets, mountain toucans, and the charismatic Andean Cock-of-the-rock; spinetails, antpittas, earthcreepers, miners, tapaculos, and cinclodes; a plethora of colorful tanager species; and many more. Some of these birds are related to familiar North American birds, but many are not. A wonderful aspect of birding in the Andes for visitors is the opportunity to get to know whole new groups of species. Another is discovering how these species groups are tied to particular habitats, and then predicting which species or genera you might find as you enter a new ecological zone. Birding in the mountains is among the most fun and rewarding of all, since the birds can change as you make just a short drive (or hike) up- or downslope.

INTRODUCTION

In recent years, Andean birding has also gotten much easier. One of the great challenges in the past was seeing the shy species that skulk in the undergrowth. Birds such as many of the rarer antpittas remained, for most people, just as illustrations in field guides, seen mostly only by researchers with mist nets and weeks or months of field time. Hummingbirds, too, are normally few and far between in the forest, and they often fly past at high speed, giving little clue as to their identity. This really began to change in the 1990s, when hummingbird feeders grew increasingly popular in areas like Mindo, Ecuador. Birds that had previously been hard to find became easy to see and photograph at locations such as the Tandayapa and Bellavista Lodges. Antpittas, though, remained elusive until a local man, Angel Paz, inherited land, created a nature reserve, and learned to attract Giant and other antpittas to worms—sometimes even feeding them by hand. This technique, since copied in many other locations, has revolutionized birding in the region and allowed many more people to see the Andes' most elusive and sought-after birds.

The overall conservation of birds and their habitats in the Andes depends on many factors, but governmental and nongovernmental protected areas, reserves run by indigenous communities, and other equivalent conserved areas will remain a keystone of conservation programs for the foreseeable future. Currently, Bolivia has 167 protected areas covering 30.87 percent of its national territory; Ecuador, 100 areas covering 23.52 percent; Colombia, 1,330 areas covering 16.4 percent; and Peru, 277 covering 22.52 percent. In total, there are 25 Endemic Bird Areas (hotspots for restricted-range birds), 403 Important Bird Areas, and 133 Alliance for Zero Extinction sites (locations where at least one Endangered or Critically Endangered species is confined to a single site) in the Andes (statistics do not include Venezuela, where the Andes cover only a small portion of the country). A key priority for bird conservation in the Andes moving forward is to ensure that protected-area and other equivalent land-conservation networks are expanded and/or sustained to include representative areas of habitat for all these priority sites, and to ensure that all Endangered and Critically Endangered birds are properly represented in the region's network of protected areas. While the impacts of climate change on the region are difficult to predict precisely, it seems clear that the more forest is lost, the more it is likely that the entire Andes–Amazon system will desiccate and be subject to more climate extremes. Reducing this loss of forest while also respecting the rights and lands of indigenous communities in the region must be a top policy priority for both national and international governments and agencies. Ensuring that protected areas have sufficient altitudinal extent to withstand future climate change is also a key conservation measure to help mitigate the impacts of desiccation and temperature rise.

As you read through this book and enjoy Owen Deutsch's magnificent photographs, we hope that you will think about visiting the Andes yourself, because, in many cases, just staying at one of the region's many ecolodges can contribute to conservation by helping to provide income for people whose livelihoods depend on ensuring that the habitat remains intact and full of birds. You can make a difference for bird conservation while enjoying birding travel!

AMERICAN BIRD CONSERVANCY IN THE ANDES

American Bird Conservancy (ABC) is a US-based nonprofit organization whose mission is to conserve wild birds and their habitats throughout the Americas. A significant part of the organization's work is dedicated to preventing the extinction of the Western Hemisphere's rarest and most endangered birds. To do this, it has been vital for ABC to develop a robust and sustainable program in the Andes, where many of South America's most endangered birds are found. The organization's work to conserve Andean birds and their habitats has the additional benefit of allowing it to help provide wintering habitat for several of the neotropical migrants that depend on the Andes during the northern winter.

ABC's work in the Andes is led primarily by partner groups in the region. ABC is a partner in the BirdLife International network and coordinates its work with both BirdLife and national partners in each country. ABC's primary partners in the Andean region include Fundación ProAves in Colombia, Fundación Jocotoco and Aves y Conservación in Ecuador, ECOAN (Asociación Ecosistemas Andinos) in Peru, and Fundación Armonía in Bolivia, among others. Together with ABC, these organizations have protected more than one million acres (including both community-operated reserves and purchased land) in more than sixty protected areas throughout the Andean nations to prevent the extinction of the region's rarest birds. In many cases, these reserves are sustained through birdwatching tourism revenues from paying guests who help to ensure that the areas can remain effectively managed and protected in the long term. Unlike many smaller ecotourism lodges, reserves run by ABC partners manage large areas of land—often purchased with donations from people like yourself. Most commercial lodges do not support large protected areas, and so by staying in lodges managed by ABC partners you can often do even more good than

INTRODUCTION

when you stay in a commercially run lodge, since, in addition to supporting jobs in nature tourism, you are also contributing to the maintenance of significant areas of critically important habitat for threatened Andean birds.

In recent years, several efforts have prioritized areas for conservation around the world, including Biodiversity Hotspots, Endemic Bird Areas, Key Biodiversity Areas, Ecoregions, and more. Major current efforts are also focused on Amazonia—primarily due to climate change concerns, with additional interests in preserving Amazonian biodiversity—and yet other initiatives aim to save certain percentages of Earth's land surface for nature. These initiatives are all important. If we truly want to conserve all biodiversity, however, we already know where we have to work, because birds point the way. Where there are threatened endemic birds, there will be other threatened and unique elements of biodiversity, and we really need to conserve viable areas that account for all of it—not just Amazonian biodiversity, not just a percentage of Earth's surface, but enough of *every* threatened ecosystem so that all birds and biodiversity can continue to exist on the planet. Acting on this philosophy, ABC has carried out a gap analysis for the most endangered birds to determine which species still lack effective protection because they are not found in any existing reserves or national parks. ABC is currently working with its partners and supporters to fill those gaps systematically to ensure that the Andean region does not experience any more bird species extinctions. More details can be found on ABC's website (www.abcbirds.org) and in ABC's Latin American Bird Reserve Network guide, available from ABC or at www.abcbirds.org/reserveguide.

In addition to its partners and the local communities with which they work, ABC would like to thank the Bobolink Foundation, The Bezos Earth Fund, The Gordon and Betty Moore Foundation, The International Conservation Fund of Canada, Rainforest Trust, The Andes Amazon Fund, World Land Trust, the Quick Response Fund for Nature, Global Affairs Canada, the Jeniam Foundation, the March Conservation Fund, the Robert Wilson Charitable Trust, Re:wild, and Gulf Coast Bird Observatory, as well as David and Patricia Davidson, Kathleen Burger and Glen Gerada, George and Cathy Ledec, and many other individual donors, for their partnership and support, which have been so vital to the success of ABC and its partners in the Andean region. Recently, ABC has entered into a partnership with BirdLife International, the National Audubon Society, Birds Canada, and the Latin American and Caribbean Network of Environmental Funds (RedLAC). Known as Conserva Aves, the partnership is designed to support the expansion of protected-area coverage for birds in Latin America and the Caribbean, including in the Andean region.

GLOSSARY FOR CAPTIONS

COUNTRY ENDEMIC A species found only within the national borders of a single country

CR Critically Endangered according to BirdLife International/IUCN (International Union for Conservation of Nature)

EN Endangered according to BirdLife International/IUCN

VU Vulnerable to extinction according to BirdLife International/IUCN

HOATZIN (*Opisthocomus hoazin*) is primarily Amazonian but also occurs along the eastern edge of the Andes up to around 3,000 feet above sea level.

THE PACIFIC SLOPE AND WESTERN ANDES | 1

OF ALL THE elements of the Andean transect, the Pacific Slope is the most ecologically varied. The western foothills and slopes vary in character immensely from north to south, driven primarily by topography and the moisture gradient—ranging from some of the world's wettest places to its driest. The northernmost extent of the western Andes lies close to the border with Panama. Moving south through Colombia, the Andes divide into three ranges. The westernmost is separated from the Cordillera Central by the Cauca Valley, an ancient rift valley now traversed by the Cauca River, which flows north to join the Magdalena River, which then discharges into the Caribbean. To the west of the Cordillera Occidental lies the wet Chocó region, which contains one of the world's most threatened lowland tropical forests. In parts of Ecuador, as much as 90 percent of this forest has already been lost or heavily degraded.

Moving farther south along the coast of Ecuador and Peru, the landscape becomes gradually drier. Some coastal areas have large mangrove forests (most commonly red mangrove), and farther inland, habitats become increasingly arid entering the Tumbesian region of southwestern Ecuador and northwestern Peru. This region is known for its variety of habitats, ranging from arid Acacia thorn forests, to moister Ceiba forests. Continuing our journey south, the area around Lima, Peru, is more desert-like, with scrubby forest mostly confined to canyons whose streams feed freshwater from the western foothills into the Pacific. Offshore, a hugely productive upwelling—driven by surface winds that allow undersea currents to bring cold water to the surface—has created one of the world's greatest marine spectacles, where millions of seabirds, particularly Guanay Cormorants and Peruvian Boobies, feed on the vast Peruvian anchoveta shoals. The anchoveta stocks in this upwelling zone unfortunately largely collapsed decades ago from overfishing. The guano from the seabirds that fed on them prior to the fishery crash became so valuable as a fertilizer that in the 1860s it provoked a war between Spain and the recently independent nation of Peru. Earlier, the Incas developed some of the world's first bird-protection laws designed to safeguard the guano which they, too, harvested as fertilizer. Further south, the landscape becomes increasingly dry as the Atacama Desert—one of the world's driest regions—takes hold.

PLATE-BILLED MOUNTAIN-TOUCAN (*Andigena laminirostris*) is one of the most striking and distinctive residents of tropical Andean cloud forests. It is found at altitudes ranging from about 3,000 feet to just over 10,000 feet in both Colombia and Ecuador. This charismatic species can frequently be seen and photographed at the Birdwatcher's House, near Mindo, Ecuador, which is run by Vinicio Perez. With patience, you can often see the birds visit the fruit feeders, where they will perch (and seem to pose for photographs) on a mossy branch.

THE CHOCÓ

GOLDEN TANAGER (*Tangara arthus*) is one of the most widespread, common, and easily seen of the cloud forest tanagers. It is commonly found in mixed flocks and is probably the most distinctive and easily identified bird in these groups. Golden Tanagers regularly attend fruit feeders, and while they can be seen easily at many locations, Mashpi Amagusa, in the Chocó of Ecuador, is among the best places to photograph them.

THE CHOCÓ > BIOGEOGRAPHY AND HISTORY

The Chocó extends from coastal northern Colombia into Ecuador. It is a relatively narrow belt of wet lowland rain forest that is both high in endemic species and highly degraded. The forests of the Chocó can be seen as a western counterpart to Amazonia in terms of biodiversity and ecology. The rainfall here is among the highest in the world, with more than forty feet of annual precipitation in some areas. The remaining large trees are often draped with epiphytes and lianas. Common trees include *Cecropias*, *Ingas*, and *Cordia*. Forests at higher elevations (usually farther inland) also have many trees and bushes in the Melastomataceae family, which produce fruit that is eaten and dispersed by birds such as manakins, tanagers, and other frugivores. Because the area has such perfect conditions for biodiversity, because it is relatively limited in extent in comparison to Amazonia, and because it is so highly degraded, this region is among the highest conservation priority forests on Earth.

The region's endemic birds tend to group into somewhat overlapping low-, mid-, and higher-elevation clusters (for example, Choco Toucan and Banded Ground-Cuckoo; Moss-backed Tanager and Black Solitaire; and Tanager Finch and Plate-billed Mountain-Toucan, respectively), and groupings in both Colombia and Ecuador are unique to, or at least primarily restricted to, those countries (for example, of two related species of *Bangsia* tanagers, Gold-ringed Tanager is found only in Colombia, and Moss-backed Tanager is mostly restricted to Ecuador). Higher elevations of the Chocó—for example, around and above Mindo, Tandayapa Valley, and Bellavista, Ecuador—blend into Andean Cloud Forest that has a similar character to much of the East Slope montane cloud forests. Note that in northern Colombia the Chocó also extends somewhat to the east of the Western Cordillera (connecting to the Nechí Lowlands), and this area has some interesting birds and biodiversity confined to it, including, for example, the Critically Endangered Chestnut-capped Piha, which can be found at ProAves Colombia's Arrierito Antioqueño Reserve, in Antioquia. It is worth noting that in Ecuador, in addition to the transition to cloud forest at higher elevations west of Quito (for example, on the higher slopes of Volcán Pichincha), areas farther south also have a distinct Chocó-like character—places such as Fundación Jocotoco's Buenaventura Reserve, for example. This is a great place to watch Long-wattled Umbrellabirds lekking and to find birds like the Club-winged Manakin and Green-crowned Brilliant; both species also have strong Chocó associations.

The Colombian Department of Chocó is one of the poorest in the country. Due to the topography and high rainfall, the area remains relatively remote from Medellín, which is the nearest large city. The department's residents are primarily Afro-Colombians descended from slaves brought to South America by the Spanish following colonization, as well as the Emberá, an indigenous group that depends on hunting and fishing and lives primarily along interior rivers. Farther south in Ecuador, Afro-Colombians migrated from the north to join the indigenous Chachi (Cayapa) people in the coastal parts of Esmeraldas Province who themselves were refugees from the Andes, pushed into the lowlands during the Spanish invasion. As with the Colombian Chocó, these communities still tend to be extremely poor and depend on subsistence agriculture for their livelihoods.

GREEN-CROWNED BRILLIANT (*Heliodoxa jacula*) is restricted to the western slope in Ecuador but is more widespread in Colombia and into Central America. These large hummingbirds can be numerous at feeders, such as those at Jocotoco's Buenaventura Reserve in Ecuador.

THE CHOCÓ > BIRD DIVERSITY AND SPECIALTIES

The Chocó has the most endemic birds of any equivalent area in the Americas, thirteen of which are named for it—the Choco Poorwill, Tinamou, Screech-Owl, Tapaculo, Toucan, Black-throated Trogon, Manakin, Elaenia, Tyrannulet, Sirystes, Woodpecker, Vireo, and Warbler. This is especially impressive given that this area lies on a continent, rather than within an island group. eBird hotspots in the region frequently have species lists in excess of four hundred, with a mix of primary- and secondary-forest species present. During the northern winter, endemic species clades are augmented by arriving neotropical migrants, including Summer Tanagers, Swainson's Thrushes, Canada and Blackburnian Warblers, Broad-winged Hawks, and many more.

Hummingbird diversity is especially marked in this region, with several endemic species, such as the spectacular Velvet-purple Coronet, Violet-tailed Sylph, and Gorgeted Sunangel. Other sought-after species include the Tanager Finch, Beautiful Jay, White-booted Racket-tail, Hoary Puffleg, Ocellated Tapaculo (found at the higher elevations and slightly more widespread), Club-winged Manakin, and Long-wattled Umbrellabird. The region basically pushes most birding superlatives to the maximum with its incredible diversity of spectacular species. It is a birding paradise but unfortunately also one of the most threatened ecosystems on Earth.

WHITE-BOOTED RACKET-TAIL (*Ocreatus underwoodii*) is surely one of the most charismatic of all Andean birds. Small yet pugnacious, with a crazy tail and white puffy "boots," it is a common and widespread species at mid-elevations from Venezuela to Bolivia. This species was previously considered conspecific with the Peruvian Racket-tail, which has cinnamon-colored boots instead of the white boots found in this species. The females are very different from the males, lacking the tail rackets and having white underparts streaked with green. Fortunately for birders, this wonderful species is commonly found at hummingbird feeders.

CONSERVATION > THE CHOCÓ

RED-HEADED BARBET (*Eubucco bourcierii*) is a striking and strongly sexually dimorphic species (female pictured) found in lowland and foothill forest from Colombia to Peru. It is found on both slopes of the Andes, although it reaches to lower altitudes in western Ecuador than it does on the eastern slope. Red-headed Barbets often forage in pairs on fruits or by seeking out insects among hanging dead leaves, and they can also occasionally be seen at fruit feeders. They are members of a group of similar closely related, stunning species that also includes the Versicolored Barbet and Lemon-throated Barbet.

The Chocó Endemic Bird Area has the largest number of restricted-range birds (more than fifty) of any Endemic Bird Area in the Americas. It contains thirty-two Important Bird Areas, and fifteen of its restricted-range birds are considered to be globally threatened. The most concerning of these are Turquoise-throated Puffleg, which is Critically Endangered (and may actually be extinct), and the Baudo Guan, Colorful Puffleg, and Banded Ground-Cuckoo, which are Endangered. Vulnerable species include the Dark-backed Wood-Quail, Plumbeous Forest-Falcon, Yellow-headed Manakin, Long-wattled Umbrellabird, Munchique Wood-Wren, Red-bellied Grackle; and Yellow-green, Black-and-gold, and Gold-ringed Tanagers, as well as Scarlet-breasted and Turquoise Dacnis.

This area has probably suffered from deforestation by percentage of land cover more than any other major ecosystem in the Andes. Part of this stems from land clearance from small farming communities, but commercial-scale logging is also ongoing at least in parts of northwestern Ecuador at the time of writing. It is, of course, possible that forestry can be conducted on a sustainable basis, but the sheer volume of large trees being removed each day suggests that this is not the case here. At least 40 percent of the Chocó forests has already been lost overall, but in some areas, such as the lowlands of northwestern Ecuador, losses are more like 90 percent or even higher. After the forest is removed, it is often replaced with crops such as cacao, oil palm, and balsa (at one point partly driven by demand for material to make wind turbine blades). Important protected areas include the Cotacachi-Cayapas Ecological Reserve in Ecuador (much of which is remote and slightly upslope of the main lowland Chocó forest area), as well as the relatively new coastal Bajo Baudó Reserve in Colombia. Fundación Jocotoco's Canandé Reserve, supported in part by American Bird Conservancy, is becoming increasingly important both as it grows in size and as it connects the lowlands to the higher slopes of Cotacachi-Cayapas. This Chocó-to-cloud forest transect is already a vital conservation corridor, acting as both a climate refuge and a critical protected area for some of the region's endemic species.

BIRDING AND PHOTOGRAPHY SITES  THE CHOCÓ

This region has many excellent birding sites. It is probably better to consider the Chocó in two separate sections: the Colombian Chocó, where, for example, Baudo Guan, Gold-ringed Tanager, and Choco Vireo can be found, and the Chocó of northwestern Ecuador, where birds such as the Moss-backed Tanager and Dark-backed Wood-Quail can be seen (although there is a good amount of cross-border overlap for most of the species). In Ecuador, one of the best ways to see some of the Chocó endemics is to set out from Quito and drive around to the west side of Volcán Pichincha and begin birding the Mindo area, then work your way northwest (and downslope) to reach the Canandé Reserve managed by Fundación Jocotoco. This route includes some of the best cloud forest birding sites in the Andes, and many of these are set up especially for birders and bird photographers. Sites in the immediate vicinity of Mindo include Paz de las Aves, with its famous antpitta-feeding operation developed by Angel Paz, which allows visitors to see Giant Antpitta, Moustached Antpitta, Chestnut-crowned Antpitta, Ochre-breasted Antpitta, and Yellow-breasted Antpitta—species that without the feeding stations would be nearly impossible for many visiting birders to see. On your way to Mindo, consider stopping at the small but mighty Zuroloma Reserve for antpittas and hummingbirds (including, occasionally, the rare Black-breasted Puffleg) and at Jocotoco's Yanacocha Reserve for higher-altitude species, such as the Great Sapphirewing, Shining Sunbeam, and the near-mythic Imperial Snipe (note that advance planning may be needed to see this species). Many of the hotels in the area have hummingbird feeders, and these attract a wide variety of species, including coronets, racket-tails, and sylphs. The Birdwatcher's House run by Vinicio Perez is a great place to see Plate-billed Mountain-Toucans as well as Toucan Barbets and many other species. Mashpi Amagusa nearby attracts a number of Chocó endemics, such as Moss-backed Tanager. Farther downslope in the Chocó Foothill Forest, the Milpe area has a nice lodge, and the illuminated moth-attracting sheet feeders there are sometimes visited by Banded Ground-Cuckoos. The nearby Canandé Reserve operated by Fundación Jocotoco conserves more than 14,000 acres of Chocó Lowland Rain Forest. The facilities are first-rate, and the site preserves some of the best remaining Chocó forest areas. Several Chocó species are hard to see in Ecuador or are present only in Colombia. These include the striking Gold-ringed Tanager and the aptly named Choco Vireo. A great place to catch up with these species is at ProAves' Las Tángaras Reserve, which is about a five-hour drive from Medellín. Both of these species, along with many other typical Chocó birds and neotropical migrants such the Canada Warbler, can be found here. These are just a few of the many great birding areas in the region. It is always worth looking at eBird hotspots and bird tour company itineraries while planning a trip, as you may find sites that better suit your itinerary or preferences.

MOSS-BACKED TANAGER (*Bangsia edwardsi*) is endemic to the wet Chocó forests along the western Andean slopes of Ecuador and Colombia at altitudes from about 1,000 to 6,000 feet. It is a hefty, bull-necked species, reminiscent of a barbet, that can appear sluggish in the field, often lingering almost motionless on a branch or close to a feeder. This and its sister species, the Gold-ringed Tanager (*Bangsia aureocincta*) of the central Colombian Chocó, have a unique appearance and color scheme that is unlike those of other tanagers. Combined with their size and behavior, these features make these unusual tanagers nearly unmistakable. The Moss-backed Tanager is a quintessential species of the wet northwestern Ecuadorian foothills, where it is easily found at birding sites such as Mashpi Amagusa, where this and other Chocó endemics have become habituated to feeders and are readily seen and photographed.

SUMMER TANAGER (*Piranga rubra*) is a boreal migrant that winters in the Chocó and nests in the southern and southwestern United States. Their *pituck* calls are often heard in the humid western-slope forests. Typically, fewer fully bright red males are seen than patchily colored young males and females.

PACIFIC TUFTEDCHEEK (*Pseudocolaptes johnsoni*) is restricted to humid forest in a narrow band along the western slope of Ecuador and Colombia up to about 5,500 feet in altitude. These charismatic birds can be found searching for insects along the moss-covered branches of trees or at their nest sites—which, for example, can be in a hole in a large bamboo trunk. This species was formerly considered a subspecies of the more northerly Buffy Tuftedcheek.

GIANT ANTPITTA (*Grallaria gigantea*) is the largest of the antpittas and has a restricted range in Ecuador and southern Colombia. As a result, BirdLife International considers it to be globally Vulnerable to extinction. These charismatic birds generally stick to the ground or low foliage and bounce along the forest floor seeking earthworms and other invertebrates. **VU**

TURQUOISE JAY (*Cyanolyca turcosa*) is a striking mid-elevation species that is common at the right altitude on both slopes of the Andes from Colombia to Peru. These animated birds tend to move through the forest in active groups, searching for insects and fruit. In the Mindo area of Ecuador, they have become habituated to moth feeders and, for example, can sometimes be seen and photographed just after dawn at the Birdwatcher's House. The species is often most easily located by its variety of calls, some of which are reminiscent of those made by the White-capped Tanager.

GREEN THORNTAIL (*Discosura conversii*) is a small, distinctive hummingbird found on the Pacific Slope from Costa Rica in the north to western Ecuador in the south—where it is strongly associated with the Chocó. Like sylphs and racket-tails, male and female thorntails are strongly dimorphic, and can seem like different species at first glance. This bird is being fed by hand using a non-native ginger flower at Punto Ornitológico Mindo, where children are encouraged to interact with hummingbirds.

YELLOW-BREASTED ANTPITTA (*Grallaria flavotincta*) is found in dense humid forest in both Colombia and Ecuador. Despite being poorly known and having a restricted range, the species is not considered to be globally endangered. Until recently, it was especially difficult to see but now can be reliably found coming to hand-fed worms at Paz de las Aves, near Mindo in Ecuador.

SMOKE-COLORED PEWEE (*Contopus fumigatus*) is widespread in mixed habitats on both slopes of the Andes from Venezuela to Chile. The species often perches conspicuously to hunt insects, sallying out and then returning to the same perch in the manner of flycatchers like the North American-breeding Eastern Wood-Pewee. This species is often first noticed by its *pip-pip* call, reminiscent of an Olive-sided Flycatcher. These birds sometimes attend moth feeders—feeding on insects attracted to the lights— at locations such as the Birdwatcher's House, near Mindo, Ecuador.

GLISTENING-GREEN TANAGER (*Chlorochrysa phoenicotis*) is an unusual tanager that is confined to the western slope of the Colombian and northern Ecuadorian Andes and is found at altitudes up to about 7,000 feet. One of the most brilliantly colored birds of the Andes, this species takes green to a whole new level. It is strongly linked to mid-elevation Chocó habitats, and these charismatic little tanagers frequently attend the fruit feeders at Mashpi Amagusa (Ecuador), which is one of the best places to see and photograph them.

EMPRESS BRILLIANT (*Heliodoxa imperatrix*) is a truly spectacular, large, slim, active hummingbird (female pictured). The males sport a long, forked tail and an inconspicuous iridescent pink throat patch. The species is found in the cloud forests of southwestern Colombia and northwestern Ecuador. While not uncommon at feeders, this species rarely perches for a photograph and visits mostly for a brief moment to feed. Fortunately, as in this case, patience eventually pays off. The species occurs only on the Pacific Slope and is found at altitudes between 1,200 and 6,000 feet.

TAWNY-BREASTED FLYCATCHER

(*Myiobius villosus*) is found on both slopes in the low- to mid-story of humid forest at altitudes up to about 6,500 feet from Venezuela to Bolivia. Like other *Myiobius* flycatchers, these animated birds often accompany mixed flocks, flicking their wings and tails and showing off their yellow rumps in a manner reminiscent of Buff-rumped Warblers.

OCHRE-BREASTED ANTPITTA (*Grallaricula flavirostris*) is a small, widely distributed, but local species that resembles a diminutive, tail-less Swainson's Thrush in the field. It is found from Colombia to Bolivia on both western and eastern Andean slopes and typically at lower elevations than other members of its genus. It also occurs in Central America north to Costa Rica. This species is readily seen at Paz de las Aves, in Ecuador, where one or more individuals have become habituated to hand-fed earthworms.

GOLDEN-COLLARED HONEYCREEPER (*Iridophanes pulcherrimus*)—like other honeycreepers—is actually a small tanager. It has a slightly unusual distribution, being found along the East Slope of the Colombian, Ecuadorian, and Peruvian Andes south to Cusco, as well as on the higher slopes of the Chocó in Ecuador and Colombia. These colorful birds sometimes attend fruit feeders, and a great place to look for them is the Mashpi Amagusa Reserve, in the Ecuadorian Chocó.

FLAME-FACED TANAGER (*Tangara parzudakii*) is one of the most striking of the small *Tangara* species. It is widespread, ranging from close to the Colombia–Venezuela border in the north to southern Peru in the south. It is found on both slopes of the Andes, and the intensity of the red and orange on the head varies slightly between populations. These colorful birds can often be found in mixed flocks of tanagers and other birds moving through the cloud forest canopy, or gathering at fruit feeders to take advantage of bananas and other food placed by lodge operators to attract them. They are found at altitudes from 4,000 feet to about 8,000 feet and occur commonly at locations such as Mashpi Amagusa, in the Ecuadorian Chocó, and Abra Patricia, on the Peruvian East Slope. Due to the large range and relative abundance of the species, it is not considered to be globally threatened.

OCHRE-BREASTED TANAGER (*Chlorothraupis stolzmanni*) is found in the foothill forests of western Ecuador and Colombia at altitudes up to about 5,000 feet. It is not a strongly marked species, being mostly olive with a large dark bill, and is usually found in lower-growth vegetation and along forest edge.

ROSE-FACED PARROT (*Pyrilia pulchra*) is a noisy and conspicuous species that is nevertheless usually hard to see well, except in areas where they are habituated to people, such as at Mashpi Amagusa, in Ecuador. The species is found at altitudes up to about 4,000 feet in humid forest on the western slopes of both Ecuador and Colombia.

VELVET-PURPLE CORONET (*Boissonneaua jardini*) is largely endemic to the wet Chocó region of western Colombia and Ecuador. It is one of the most spectacular of the region's hummingbirds and one of the most aggressive. The species is common around hummingbird feeders, such as those in the Mindo area of Ecuador, where it can become habituated to people and may even land on observers' fingers or cell phones. Like other coronets, this species is prone to raising its wings upon landing, exposing its cinnamon underwing coverts. While it can appear fairly unremarkable while perched, in the right light, this species' iridescent purple, green, and blue hues are stunning. The white outer tail feathers complete a most dramatic appearance, which is surely among the most attractive and charismatic of all hummingbirds. Velvet-purple Coronet is not yet considered globally threatened but appears to be declining, despite still being relatively abundant within its restricted global range.

The striking **BLACK-CHINNED MOUNTAIN TANAGER** (*Anisognathus notabilis*) is restricted to the upper levels of the Chocó and Pacific Slope from about 3,000 feet to just over 7,000 feet in altitude. While it superficially resembles a Blue-winged Mountain Tanager, it has a distinctly oriole-like countenance in the field and is generally found at lower altitudes than the aforementioned species.

CRIMSON-RUMPED TOUCANET (*Aulacorhynchus haematopygus*) is a distinctive and charismatic species found in northeastern Colombia, along the Western and Central Cordilleras of the Colombian Andes, and into western Ecuador. Toucans and toucanets have a habit of forming groups that follow each other, and they can sometimes be seen flying across canopy gaps in single file in their distinctive flap-and-glide style. These birds are omnivorous and can eat fruits and insects but will also prey on other birds.

FLAME-RUMPED TANAGER (*Ramphocelus flammigerus*) is a large, noisy, and boisterous species that frequently engages in bill-to-bill skirmishes in the vicinity of bird feeders, including those at Mashpi Amagusa, in Ecuador, where this picture was taken. Rump color on this species ranges widely from yellow to red depending on elevation and latitude, and there are hybrids among populations as well. These charismatic birds are often found in groups in which individuals in female-type plumages outnumber adult males.

GORGETED SUNANGEL (*Heliangelus amethysticollis*) is a beautifully subtle species that is almost endemic to Ecuador except for a slight incursion into southern Colombia. The species is known to attend feeders, where it appears especially short-legged as it perches, frequently flicking or holding its wings out in a distinctively drooped manner.

PURPLE-BIBBED WHITETIP (*Urosticte benjamini*) is found from central Colombia to northern Peru at altitudes up to about 5,000 feet. Males are distinctive because of a curious and obvious white subterminal tail spot, while females are strongly streaked with green below. This species is commonly found attending feeders at sites including Mashpi Amagusa, in the Chocó of western Ecuador.

RUFOUS-THROATED TANAGER (*Ixothraupis rufigula*) is endemic to the Chocó region of northwestern Ecuador and western Colombia. It is found in cloud forest at altitudes up to about 7,000 feet and also commonly attends fruit feeders at locations such as Mashpi Amagusa—which is an excellent place to see and photograph the species.

COLLARED ARACARI (pronounced ara-sari) (*Pteroglossus torquatus*) is widespread across the northern Andes. These photos shows the pale-mandibled form, which is the southernmost subspecies.

MOUSTACHED ANTPITTA (*Grallaria alleni*) is a poorly known species that BirdLife International considers to be Vulnerable to extinction. It is very similar to the Scaled Antpitta but is found at slightly higher elevations, has a different song, and differs somewhat in appearance—showing a reduced pale upper breast band. It is found patchily through central Colombia to northern Ecuador and can be seen fairly reliably coming to hand-fed worms at Paz de las Aves, near Mindo in Ecuador. VU

VIOLET-TAILED SYLPH (*Aglaiocercus coelestis*) is a striking, long-tailed hummingbird that occurs at middle elevations in western Ecuador and Colombia. Caught in the right light, the forked tail has an otherworldly violet-blue hue that can seem to shimmer. The length of the male's tail in comparison to the bird's body is remarkable, as is the difference between the male and female. (The female lacks the long tail and has a whitish breast and chestnut belly.) The similar male Long-tailed Sylph lacks the violet-blue throat patch of the Violet-tailed, and its tail has a blue-green sheen. The Long-tailed is found primarily on the East Slope and at higher elevations, but there can be overlap. While feeding at either a flower or feeder, Violet-tailed Sylphs typically perch or cling, rather than hovering. They are commonly found at feeders, and while they are not shy, they can be hard to photograph well, due to their proportions and because the tail is rarely splayed in good light.

VARIABLE SEEDEATER (*Sporophila corvina*) is found from Central America to western Colombia and Ecuador. In the northern part of its range, males are predominantly black, whereas more southerly birds show variable quantities of white on the underparts. These appealing seed eaters are often found in grassy areas of the western lowlands and foothills, along with other species of seedeater and seed-finch.

VIOLET-BELLIED HUMMINGBIRD (*Chlorestes julie*) is found from Panama to western Ecuador in lowland forest and clearings up to about 3,600 feet in altitude. The male has the appearance of a small woodnymph, but note the red base of the lower mandible. These attractive, small hummingbirds can sometimes be seen at feeders.

MASKED WATER-TYRANT (*Fluvicola nengeta*) has an unusual and disjunct distribution, occurring in western Ecuador and extreme southern Colombia, as well as in eastern Brazil. These smart-looking, charismatic flycatchers can often be seen near water. They can often occur in urban and other developed areas.

CROWNED WOODNYMPH (*Thalurania colombica*) is widespread from Belize to Ecuador. While there is a confusing array of potential subspecies and forms with complicated mixtures of morphology—especially in Colombia—the northernmost individuals of this species typically have a violet crown, while the southernmost have a green crown, as can be seen on this bird, photographed in northwestern Ecuador.

> **FROM THE FIELD** — *Personal stories from the leaders of American Bird Conservancy's primary bird and habitat conservation partners in the tropical Andes.*

SCALING UP PROTECTED AREAS TO CONSERVE AND RESTORE ECUADOR'S BIRDS AND BIODIVERSITY

THE TROPICAL ANDES are the place to be for a birder. Unparalleled in the diversity of birds, the tropical Andes surpass all other regions in the number of endemic birds and, sadly, also in the number of areas acutely threatened. It is here where we can all make the biggest difference. The tropical Andes are thus the place to be for everyone who cares about biodiversity.

Against the odds (89 percent extinction probability), Fundación Jocotoco has saved Critically Endangered birds from extinction. Through dedicated efforts, we quadrupled the population of the Pale-headed Brushfinch in just nine years. Today, we are replicating such efforts on a much larger scale, restoring the ecosystem of an entire island, Floreana, in the Galápagos. That restoration allows us to reintroduce twelve locally extinct species (including one that survives only in captivity today). Hence, the population of Floreana Mockingbirds is likely to increase strongly in the coming years.

While developing specific actions is important for species with critically low population sizes, it is generally sufficient to protect nature in the tropical Andes by allowing the habitat to recover by itself. The ensuing ecosystem recovery is both rapid and complete. In the tropical rain forest, we see that animals across all groups (from insects to amphibians, birds, and mammals) return to once-degraded land in a diversity that matches that of old-growth forests within just one human generation (twenty-five years). Often, however, the recovery of species is even faster than that. The population of endemic birds such as the Ecuadorian Hillstar increased eight- to tenfold in Jocotoco's Chakana Reserve within just twelve years. These data show that our protection works. By extension, we, as humans, can protect the species we love. This is the good news that younger generations need.

Jocotoco has evolved from being a local organization focused on protecting species within our seventeen reserves (totalling one hundred thousand acres currently) to one focused on regional conservation outcomes. By expanding our reserves and working with communities, Jocotoco establishes effective buffer zones for national parks. Our strategy works; it saves very large regions, reconnects wildlife populations, and enables climate adaptation. Endangered endemic birds have shifted their distributional ranges by almost 1,000 feet in elevation within thirty years. Species' ranges change, ecosystems change, and we humans also need climate adaptation. Increasing the scale and elevational span of protected areas is thus paramount. It provides climate adaptation and water, cools the climate, and reduces soil erosion. The return of megafauna, Harpy Eagles, jaguars, spectacled bears, and mountain tapirs to areas where they were previously hunted out testifies to Jocotoco's success.

Local organizations such as Jocotoco present the most effective and efficient way to achieve conservation successes jointly with our international partners, such as American Bird Conservancy. We protect more than 10 percent of all the species of birds in the world. Working with authorities and communities, we helped achieve the declaration of a marine protected area encompassing twenty-three thousand square miles, linking the Galápagos with Costa Rica. This is an important swim-way for threatened sharks, marine turtles, rays, and whales. Thus, Jocotoco protects not only migratory bird species by saving their overwintering and staging sites—from the windswept páramo for Buff-breasted Sandpipers and Baird's Sandpipers to the subtropical forests shrouded in mist, where Canada Warblers and Cerulean Warblers spend their winters—but also migratory fish, marine mammals, and turtles.

North American migratory birds require support from various organizations across their life cycles. Similarly, protecting nature in the tropical Andes requires multilevel support, from the birders who visit Jocotoco's reserves and beautiful lodges to individual and institutional donors and companies that back nature-positive solutions. Jointly, we can restore hope by protecting very significant proportions of global biodiversity.

MARTIN SCHAEFER
Chief Executive Officer, Fundación Jocotoco

COLLARED ARACARI (*Pteroglossus torquatus*) of which the pale-mandibled form (pictured) is endemic to the Ecuadorian Chocó. They frequently nest in abandoned woodpecker holes such as this one at Punto Ornitológico Mindo. They primarily feed on fruits, but will also eat small lizards, as well as the eggs or nestlings of other birds. The species is regularly found at the Canandé Reserve managed by Fundación Jocotoco.

TUMBESIA AND THE MARAÑÓN VALLEY

WHITE-TIPPED DOVE (*Leptotila verreauxi*) is one of the most widespread neotropical species, occurring from Argentina in the south to the United States in the north—where it reaches South Texas and, occasionally, Arizona. The species is usually split into three main groups; birds in the Marañón region are part of the *decolor* group that extends into Ecuador and shows pink (rather than bluish) skin around the eye.

TUMBESIA AND THE MARAÑÓN VALLEY > BIOGEOGRAPHY AND HISTORY

The Tumbesian biogeographic region lies between the wet Chocó to its north and the deserts of the central Peruvian coast to the south. It is named for the Tumbes Department of Peru, but it also includes parts of the El Oro and Azuay provinces of Ecuador, as well as areas to their north—and parts of the Piura, Lambayeque, and La Libertad Departments of Peru to the south. The region has distinct wet and dry seasons and is typified by Tumbesian Thornscrub but also has larger trees, such as Ceibas and mesquite, as well as cacti, which together form an open forest known as Pacific Dry Deciduous Forest—because most of the trees lose their leaves in the dry season. The Marañón River, often cited as one of the main sources of the Amazon, originates from the Lauricocha and Nupe Rivers, which meet close to the village of Rondos, in northern Peru. Before the river flows into the Ucayali farther east, the deep Marañón Valley acts as a barrier to wildlife movement and serves the important ecological function of separating species lineages between the northern and central Andes. Multiple dam projects are proposed for the river, but questions remain about both their necessity and their ecological impact.

While the Tumbesian region is most typically associated with dry thorn forest, it in fact has a large range of habitat types and hence a significant diversity of birds, including many endemic species. Major Tumbesian bird-habitat groupings are associated either with deciduous forest dominated by Acacias and Ceibas (typically *C. trichistandra*) at altitudes up to about 4,000 feet or with semievergreen Ceiba forest (typically *C. pentandra*) above that altitude. Lying entirely within northwestern Peru, the Marañón Valley is typified by arid Central Andean Thornscrub, with riparian Marañón Deciduous Forest and some irrigated agriculture, including orchards—around Balsas, for example. In this area, the river carves out a deep canyon that makes for a spectacular drive as the road winds up the steep switchbacks to the east. Areas to the west of the Marañón are distinctly more arid, and the dry valley itself lies in the rain shadow of mountains to its east—the lower sections being characterized by columnar cacti such as *Browningia*, as well as Acacias and dry, low-lying, scrubby vegetation. Farther north from the deepest part of the canyon, around the town of Bagua, the Marañón habitats are more varied, and the higher slopes start to include more humid forest, including stunted cloud forest. As the narrow single-track road from Balsas climbs out of the east side of the canyon toward Leimebamba, the avifauna becomes more typical of East Slope cloud forest, with birds such as Scarlet-bellied Mountain Tanager, Streaked Tuftedcheek, and even high Andean species such as Andean Flicker entering the scene.

The Tumbesian region is among the lowest sections of the Andes and includes the lowest pass across the mountains at Abra de Porculla (at about 7,000 feet), which lies about sixty miles west of Bagua. The origins of the name Tumbes are uncertain, but the region does have a rich though somewhat conflicted history. The region was absorbed under Incan rule in the 1400s but was also the place where the Spanish first entered Peru in 1532 before starting the war and ensuing colonization that ultimately ended the Incan Empire (which itself was—by that point—already somewhat weakened by internal conflict). Parts of this region also include territory that was historically disputed between Ecuador and Peru, although this dispute was formally ended in 1998 with a border agreement ratified by both nations. Following opposition to oil development on indigenous lands in Amazonia, clashes between police and activists in 2009 resulted in the deaths of thirty-one people—both police and indigenous representatives—near Bagua. The Peruvian Congress ultimately repealed the regulations that had initially led to the protests. To the east of the Marañón, the Chachapoyan culture was originally centered around the Utcubamba Valley and its environs. Relatively little is recorded about the Chachapoyans, yet the ancient, abandoned, walled settlement at Kuélap is second only to Machu Picchu in terms of its preservation and complexity. A recently opened cable-car system allows visitors greater access to the ruins, which previously required a two-hour drive or a long hike from the main road. The Chachapoyans were conquered by the Incas but apparently never settled well under Incan rule. One of their enduring cultural legacies are the unusual burial urns used to house their desiccated dead, which have the appearance of large decorative vases. The region once home to the Chachapoyans is also known as the home of one of the world's tallest waterfalls at Gocta, with an overall drop of 2,500 feet. The waterfall was little known outside of the immediate area until relatively recently.

UNIFORM ANTSHRIKE (*Thamnophilus unicolor*) is a bird of the east Andean slope, where it is found in the understory of cloud forest and in surrounding scrubby areas up to about 7,500 feet in altitude. The male is truly nondescript, and the female (pictured) has only slightly more variety in coloration (adding brown to the male's gray). The species tends to occupy more humid forests surrounding the drier valleys of the region. The Abra Patricia Reserve in northern Peru, operated by ECOAN, is a good place to see this plain but nevertheless subtly beautiful species.

TUMBESIA AND THE MARAÑÓN VALLEY — BIRD DIVERSITY AND SPECIALTIES

The diversity of birds in this region is staggering. There are dozens of restricted-range endemics, several with tiny global ranges, and a vast diversity of habitats, ranging from coastal beaches and mangroves to arid rocky desert, scrub and thorn forest, humid upland forest, fast-flowing streams, and deep cactus-filled canyons. It is a birding paradise, and it lies adjacent to additional amazing birding areas, such as the Alto Mayo region in Peru and Podocarpus National Park in Ecuador. This is really among the best places on Earth for bird diversity, and it is difficult to know where to start given the amazing variety of families and species present here. While there is much crossover, the birds can be loosely divided into three main groups: those that are associated chiefly with arid, primarily coastal areas largely comprised of dry thorn forests and Acacias; those that are associated with more humid inland and upland forests; and those that are endemic to the Marañón region. The former includes characteristic birds such as the Peruvian Plantcutter, Rufous Flycatcher, Scarlet-backed Woodpecker, Superciliated Wren, Tumbes Tyrant, White-tailed Jay, and Baird's Flycatcher. The next group includes birds such as the Blackish-headed Spinetail, Slaty Becard, Henna-hooded Foliage-gleaner, and Gray-cheeked Parakeet. In terms of Marañón specialties, the Marañon Crescentchest, Yellow-faced Parrotlet, Chestnut-backed Thornbird, Great Spinetail, Gray-winged Inca-Finch, and Buff-bellied Tanager are good examples of the characteristic species.

Many more wide-ranging birds can also be found in the region. For example, Fasciated Tiger-Herons are often seen along fast-moving rivers such as the Utcubamba. Lesser Nighthawks can be found in the region (whether these are resident, migratory, or both needs confirmation), and King Vultures are sometimes seen gliding and circling high overhead—there are hundreds of species to be found. It is possible to build a significant bird list, including many of the endemics and specialties, by beginning close to the coast and driving a transect east all the way across the Andes.

JOHNSON'S TODY-FLYCATCHER (*Poecilotriccus luluae*) is endemic to an area south of the Marañón between roughly 6,000 and 9,500 feet in altitude, where it is particularly fond of patches of bamboo and shrubs where the forest has been disturbed by landslides. The species was first found by Ned Johnson, who proposed naming it the "Lulu's Tody-Tyrant," but the name was changed both to honor his memory and because members of the South American Classification Committee did not think that Lulu was an appropriate name for a bird. COUNTRY ENDEMIC (PERU). EN

CONSERVATION — TUMBESIA AND THE MARAÑÓN VALLEY

This region consists of two Endemic Bird Areas: the Marañón Valley and the Tumbesian region. Tumbesia has an astonishing fifty-six restricted-range bird species and forty-six Important Bird Areas, with twenty-two restricted-range birds and sixteen Important Bird Areas in the Marañón. Of the region's unique birds, fortunately, only seven are considered either Endangered or Critically Endangered. These include the Marañon Spinetail, which is Critically Endangered, and the Gray-bellied Comet, White-winged Guan, Gray-backed Hawk, El Oro Parakeet, Ecuadorian Tapaculo, and Pale-headed Brushfinch, all of which are Endangered. Many of the other restricted-range species are fortunately not of high conservation concern, but several other species are considered to be globally Vulnerable, including the Peruvian Plantcutter, Rufous Flycatcher, Esmeraldas Woodstar, Blackish-headed Spinetail, Yellow-faced Parrotlet, and Purple-backed Sunbeam. Neotropical migrants using this area include Black-billed Cuckoo, Swainson's Thrush, and Alder Flycatcher.

Significant conservation actions are already underway to prevent the extinction of the region's most endangered birds. This includes a reforestation program run by ECOAN (Asociación Ecosistemas Andinos) in Peru to create recovery habitat for the Gray-bellied Comet near its main stronghold along the Río Chonta northeast of Cajamarca. The White-winged Guan, which has historically suffered from hunting and habitat loss, is also benefiting from a reintroduction program at Chaparrí, although the wild population centered around Quebrada El Limón and its environs remains threatened. The El Oro Parakeet and Pale-headed Brushfinch have both benefited from the creation of Ecuadorian reserves by Fundación Jocotoco with support from American Bird Conservancy.

Habitat loss in this region has been severe, primarily along the coast, and has been driven mostly by agriculture, grazing, and development. Relatively few large contiguous patches of natural forest remain, and those that do are often grazed and have become at least somewhat degraded.

The eastern part of the region is in better condition, though, and a good amount of forest is present in some areas. There are currently insufficient protected areas to provide full coverage for the most threatened birds, and parks and reserves need to be expanded and new ones created. Among the most important existing protected areas in the region are Machalilla National Park in Ecuador and the Northwest Peru Biosphere Reserve. The coastal mangroves at Manglares-Churute are also important, though not ecologically unique to the Tumbesian area. Several smaller reserves operated by nongovernmental organizations complement the national protected areas in important ways—such as by providing protected habitat for birds not included in government-managed parks. These include sites such as Buenaventura and Yungilla, both managed by Fundación Jocotoco, as well as Cerro Blanco and Chaparrí. American Bird Conservancy has been active in supporting multiple reserves in this region in partnership with ECOAN and Jocotoco.

SPECKLED HUMMINGBIRD (*Adelomyia melanogenys*) is an unusual, small, mainly brown hummingbird that is deceptively attractive when seen up close. These charismatic hummingbirds are widespread in the Andes at mid-elevations and range from Venezuela to Argentina.

TUMBESIA AND THE MARAÑÓN VALLEY > BIRDING AND PHOTOGRAPHY SITES

This region has a plethora of great birding sites. Before planning any birding trip, it is always well worth both checking tour group itineraries to this part of the world and looking at eBird hotspots (at eBird.org) for key sites. It can also be helpful to make a list of target endemic birds, to make sure you are aware of all of the key species and that you have a plan to catch up with as many as possible. This is especially true in this endemic-rich area. Because so many potential options are here, I suggest that you think of this part of the world in terms of two potential birding routes.

The first would start in Guayaquil, Ecuador. While heading mostly south and east on this route, you could also start with a side trip to the Pacific Dry Deciduous Forests and Semi-Evergreen Forest of Cerro Blanco Reserve west of Guayaquil to look for birds such as the Gray-cheeked Parakeet, White-tailed Jay, Tumbes Tyrannulet, Tumbes Pewee, Blackish-headed Spinetail, Baird's Flycatcher, Henna-hooded Foliage-gleaner, Gray-backed Hawk, Short-tailed Field-Tyrant, Scarlet-backed Woodpecker, and Superciliated and Fasciated Wrens, for example. Great Green Macaws used to occur at this reserve but can now best be seen at Jocotoco's communal reserve at Las Balsas, which lies about thirty-five miles west-northwest of Guayaquil (and is a different location from the aforementioned Balsas in the Marañón Valley). To the south of Guayaquil, the route continues past the Manglares-Churute Ecological Reserve, which is a coastal mangrove area with lowland forest and a broad range of commoner neotropical birds. It has good trails and a boardwalk, as well as boat tours for visitors. Nearby flooded grasslands and marshy areas are known for birds such as Horned Screamer and Large-billed Seed-Finch, although visitors should be aware that the long grass in this area also plays host to large numbers of aggressive chiggers. The route could then continue to Fundación Jocotoco's Yunguilla Reserve. This site is the only known location for Pale-headed Brushfinch. The reserve lies about fifty miles southeast of Manglares-Churute as the Pinnated Bittern flies (although in reality, the bitterns will stay in the coastal marshes at Manglares-Churute!). For this and other Jocotoco reserves, it is always important to contact the organization in advance at www.jocotoco.org.ec to book accommodations and your reserve visit. Your route could then continue by looping in the new Jocotoco reserve for the recently discovered Blue-throated Hillstar in the Cushion Páramo of Cerro de Arcos, which lies about forty-five miles south-southwest of Yunguilla. The hillstar can be found perching on the *Puyas* and feeding on the orange *Chuquiraga* flowers around the reserve. While not strictly a Tumbesian bird, the hillstar will surely tempt most birders who are on a Tumbesian endemics swing to go off route slightly. Another forty-five miles south lies the Jorupe Reserve, which is pure Pacific Dry Deciduous Forest and has the full suite of Tumbesian birds associated with this ecosystem. Many of the species can be seen from the trail system immediately around the lodge, and this includes many of the species mentioned above for Cerro Blanco. Birds like the Slaty Becard are commonly seen here, as well as other classic Tumbesian species, such as Blackish-headed Spinetail and Henna-hooded Foliage-

TAWNY-BELLIED HERMIT (*Phaethornis syrmatophorus*) is a relatively widespread hummingbird that has a narrow Peruvian distribution extending just south of the Marañón River but, interestingly, not farther south into Peru. The species is also found north from Ecuador to Colombia, however. These large hermits have a long, white-tipped tail; a strongly curved bill; warm brown underparts; and a strongly marked face pattern, and they can sometimes be found at hummingbird feeders.

MARVELOUS SPATULETAIL

(*Loddigesia mirabilis*) is one of the world's most spectacular and unusual birds. The male's long tail spatules are used during its lekking display and seem to follow the bird around like a butterfly in flight. The species was considered Endangered until recently, and it is restricted to the Utcubamba Valley of northern Peru and its immediate environs. COUNTRY ENDEMIC (PERU)

WHITE-LINED TANAGER

(*Tachyphonus rufus*) is a widespread neotropical species that tends to prefer drier areas with secondary growth and forest edge. It is found throughout the northern Andes and ranges into Panama and Amazonia. The mostly black males contrast with the almost entirely rufous-brown females; this can be a clue to their identity, since this tanager is often found in pairs and less frequently around mixed flocks.

gleaner. While your trip in southern Ecuador could easily continue east to such sites as Tapichalaca and Copalinga, locations such as the stunted cloud forest of Utuana and the Chocó cloud forests of Buenaventura (among the most southerly areas of this habitat type) are still in the more westerly part of the region and well worth a day or two to round out the trip's bird list if you decide not to venture toward the more distant eastern locations.

In Peru, a Tumbesian and Marañón birding trip could begin in Chiclayo, near the coast, and start with a morning at the Bosque Pómac Historic Sanctuary, which lies about twenty miles northeast of the city. This site is one of the few places where it is possible to see Peruvian Plantcutter. Listen for its weird and slightly irritating and complaining buzzy calls. It is also a good site for Rufous Flycatcher and Tumbes Swallow, along with other commoner Tumbesian birds. In order to see White-winged Guan, which is one of the region's most spectacular birds, it is possible to arrive at Quebrada El Limón very early in the morning and hike up to the best forest patches, but be aware that the guans are extremely skittish here, and one would have to be extremely lucky to get a good photograph. In order to get better photos, one could instead head to Chaparrí, where the birds are being reintroduced. While these are not genuinely "wild" birds, they are breeding here independently and offer radically better photo opportunities. Chaparrí also has a range of other excellent birds, including King Vulture, and it has a spectacled bear rescue facility. From Chaparrí, there are a couple of routes to take. One route would be to head over to Abra de Porculla—which itself offers good birding and is a good site for Piura Chat-Tyrant, for example—in the direction of Jaén. The Gotas de Agua Private Reserve lies about five miles northeast of the city and is a little gem of a birding site. It is a good place to look for the stunning Marañon Crescentchest, among other birds. Heading east from here takes you in the direction of some of the world's great birding sites, such as Abra Patricia and Pomacochas, but we will tackle those later in the book, when we start down the East Slope. Part way to Abra Patricia, though, is good Marañón semihumid forest around the Gocta waterfall. This area can also be good for the crescentchest, as well as such birds as Marañon Thrush, Buff-bellied Tanager, Speckle-chested Piculet, and the Marañón subspecies of Tropical Gnatcatcher (considered a separate species by some authorities). A second route from Chaparrí could be to head toward Cajamarca and stop off at the Río Chonta to look for the rare Gray-bellied Comet before heading past Celendín and into the arid valley of the Marañón River itself. The tops of the columnar cacti here should be scanned for the awesome Yellow-faced Parrotlets that often feed on them. One time, I saw a Baird's Sandpiper on the sandy banks of the river, too. More typical birds of the dry forest and canyons are both Buff-bridled and Gray-winged Inca-Finches (both Peruvian endemics) and the Chestnut-backed Thornbird, which builds its large spiky nest in an Acacia tree using Acacia twigs for construction. From here, there are many routes to take, but almost all of them should lead you next to the Marvelous Spatuletail. See the East Slope chapter for more on that species and where to find it.

THICK-BILLED EUPHONIA (*Euphonia laniirostris*) is one of a group of widespread and similar-looking euphonia species that often confuse birders. Euphonias were once considered to be related to tanagers, but DNA work has shown that they are in fact closer to finches. The crown and throat pattern and underpart coloration, as well as distribution, can be helpful in separating the males by species. Females (above left) are often best identified based on range, by the males they consort with, or through photos.

SPARKLING VIOLETEAR (*Colibri coruscans*) is a large, widespread, and common hummingbird found at altitudes up to about 12,000 feet across the Andes. It overlaps with the similar but smaller Lesser Violetear at altitudes from about 4,000 to 9,000 feet, but the Sparkling's purplish-blue ear coverts also extend to its throat (Lesser's throat is green), and Sparkling has a much more prominent blue patch on the lower breast and belly. It is found from Venezuela to Argentina and ranges east into Brazil.

COLLARED INCA (*Coeligena torquata*) is a large, striking hummingbird that ranges from Colombia to Peru and occurs on both eastern and western Andean slopes. The species is a regular at hummingbird feeders and is found from around 6,000 to 10,000 feet in altitude.

GOLDEN GROSBEAK (*Pheucticus chrysogaster*) is a striking and unmistakable species of forest-edge and secondary habitats that is common in the Marañón region. It is widespread here in optimal habitat and is also found in Ecuador and Colombia. A great place to look for these distinctive birds is around the village of Pomacochas, in northern Peru, which is close to the area where you can also see the Marvelous Spatuletail.

WHITE-BELLIED WOODSTAR (*Chaetocercus mulsant*) is a tiny gem of a hummingbird that is most commonly found in transitional and unforested habitats of the Andes from Colombia to Bolivia (female on right). It is typically found at elevations up to 9,000 feet, and perhaps higher, and often attends feeders. Woodstars are among the smallest hummingbirds and can be mistaken for large insects at first glance. Freezing their incredibly fast wingbeats in a photo usually requires an elaborate multiflash setup.

GUANAY CORMORANT (*Leucocarbo bougainvillii*) is one of the most abundant offshore bird species in central Peru. Very large numbers nest on nearshore islands, including the Ballestas Islands, although, almost unbelievably, current numbers are greatly diminished from the historic population highs before the anchoveta fishery was depleted. The river of cormorants that forms as large flocks leave their nesting and roosting sites and file out to sea is one of the great sights of the central coast.

THE LAND OF THE NAZCA — BIOGEOGRAPHY AND HISTORY

While the Andes Mountains themselves mostly begin in earnest some miles inland from the coast, in many ways they truly begin well offshore at the Peru-Chile Trench, which is the start of the subduction zone of the Nazca Plate. While plate subduction beneath the South American continent began some 140 million years ago, the Nazca Plate itself formed about fifty million years ago as a section of the much larger Pacific Plate. This dense tectonic plate, some six million square miles in extent, is named for the Nazca people, who inhabited parts of the Peruvian coast (centered around what is now known as the city of Ica) about two thousand years ago. The Nazca Plate is colliding with the South American continent, and because it is made of denser basalt, it is sinking beneath the lighter continental plate to create what is known as a subduction zone. Deep in the Earth along its lower edge, the Nazca Plate is being driven into Earth's mantle, conducting magma toward the surface. This has resulted in the creation of about 150 active volcanoes across the Andean region. Along the length of its upper surface, the force of the plate's movement—which progresses at about three inches per year—has given rise to the mountains of the Andes, and it continues to push them skyward at a rate of about half an inch per year. This pressure causes the earth above the plate to form convoluted topographical features, hence the Andes are known as "fold mountains."

The region we are referring to as the Land of the Nazca is likely a little more extensive than that occupied by the original Nazca culture. It extends from somewhat north of Lima, Peru, to the Chilean border to the south; out to sea about fifty to one hundred miles to the Peru–Chile Trench; and inland into the first foothills and canyons of the Andes. It equates approximately to the Peruvian departments of Lima, Ica, and the coastal portions of Arequipa, Moquegua, and Tacna. The land is primarily arid, as it lies immediately north of the Atacama Desert, which just edges into southern Peru at its northern boundary. The region comprises extensive sand dunes inland, a rocky coastline with globally significant marine bird colonies on offshore islands, a series of coastal marshes, small oases in the desert, and the beginning of the Andean foothills, which are cloaked in shrubs, *Agave*, mesquite, dry scrubby thorn forest, and abundant cacti. The Atacama is the world's driest nonpolar desert. Some weather stations there have never detected rain, but to the west and north, the cold Humboldt Current hugs the Peruvian coast and creates a blanket of winter coastal fog by condensing the humid tropical air above—which is known as *garúa* in Peru and *camanchaca* in Chile—and this can support vegetation that is hydrated by the airborne water droplets. Such vegetated areas are most prominent on coastal hills that gather fog and are known as *lomas* (Spanish for "hills"). Along with coastal marshes and riparian vegetation flanking rivers feeding the Pacific, these are often the only natural green areas in this otherwise sandy, desertified landscape. Typical vegetation in this region includes *Euphorbia* shrubs, ground bromeliads, and halophytic bushes, with Tamarugo (*Prosopis*) trees on dry foothill slopes with slightly more rainfall. Roughly every four to seven years, due to changes in atmospheric pressure, a warm current known as El Niño or El Niño de Navidad ("the Christmas Child") replaces the Humboldt Current off the coast, serving to boost ocean temperatures. This causes the region to experience unusually large amounts of rainfall and a resurgence in vegetation, including flowering blooms in the desert.

The Nazca civilization itself is probably most famous for the Nazca Lines, which adorn the desert about 220 miles south of Lima. The lines depict giant images, including some of birds, and can be appreciated properly only from the air—presumably something that the Nazca people themselves were unable to do. The Nazca culture, which followed on from the Paracas culture that preceded it, is also known for its woven textiles, pottery, pyramids, and irrigation systems known as *puquios*. These were so well constructed that about thirty of them are still in use today.

SURFBIRD (*Calidris virgata*) is a boreal migrant that nests in Alaska and northwestern Canada and winters along the Pacific coast south to central Chile and Tierra del Fuego. These stout shorebirds are well named, as they spend much of their lives foraging on rocks within feet of the splashing waves.

BIRD DIVERSITY AND SPECIALTIES ⟩ THE LAND OF THE NAZCA

Bird diversity along the Peruvian coast is relatively high and includes a mixture of migratory species that breed in the Northern Hemisphere, such as the Whimbrel and Franklin's Gull, as well as birds with an Andean lineage, such as the Least Seedsnipe and Grassland Yellow-Finch. Seabirds such as Inca Terns and Peruvian Boobies and the near-endemic Peruvian Diving-Petrel, as well as desert species such as the Coastal Miner, are also found here. Along with the Black-necked Woodpecker, Surf Cinclodes, and Cactus Canastero, which are also found in this area, the miner is endemic to Peru.

Interestingly, it is likely that the rare Ringed Storm-Petrel almost certainly nests somewhere in the vicinity of Lima, but the exact nesting areas there have yet to be located. We believe they breed there because downed storm-petrels, apparently confused by building lights, are found regularly around the city. The species' nesting areas in the Atacama Desert farther south have recently been found, as have those of the Markham's Storm-Petrel, another rare seabird that can be seen in Peruvian waters off the coast of Lima. Some of the rare breeding seabirds of the Galápagos Islands—such as the Waved Albatross and Swallow-tailed Gull—also regularly find their way to these waters, along with birds such as Red-necked Phalaropes, some of which were astonishingly tracked to Scotland, where they nest. The central Peruvian coast also has an unusual localized sooty form of the Vermillion Flycatcher that can be seen around Lima (at the Villa wetlands, on the coast south of the city, for example).

Other residents of coastal marshes like Pantanos de Villa include marsh birds such as the (very) Wren-like Rushbird and Many-colored Rush Tyrant, both of which can be found in reedy areas that are dominated by totora, a form of giant bulrush sedge, as well as shorebirds such as Stilt and Baird's Sandpipers, which can occasionally be found in the shallower pools. Other predominant plants in these coastal marshes include *Typha*, *Phragmites*, *Grama*, and *Salicornia*. In drier open areas, Burrowing Owls and Peruvian Thick-knees can be seen. A similar list of species can be found at the El Paraíso and Ventanilla wetlands that lie about seventy miles north and ten miles north of Lima, respectively, as well as among the scattered coastal marshes that flank the west side of the Pan-American Highway as it hugs the coast to the south. Small towns and oases can be good places to find the Oasis Hummingbird, the spectacular Peruvian Sheartail, and, potentially, the rare Peruvian Martin. West Peruvian Doves are abundant close to the coast, and both American and Blackish Oystercatchers are found on sandy and rocky beaches, respectively. Harbors such as the one in Pisco often attract flocks of gulls, including Belcher's, Gray, and Gray-hooded Gull, as well as Peruvian Pelicans.

⟨ INCA TERN (*Larosterna inca*) is one of the most distinctive and charismatic of this region's seabirds. It is fortunately common and hard to miss—one can even find Inca Terns nesting on La Rosa Náutica restaurant, on the pier below Miraflores in Lima, where many visitors begin or end their trip to the Peruvian Andes. The species' bright red bill, yellow facial skin, and white whiskers make this unique tern virtually unmistakable.

CONSERVATION — THE LAND OF THE NAZCA

This region roughly equates to BirdLife International's Peru-Chile Slope Endemic Bird Area (EBA). EBAs are defined as areas where two or more bird species with global ranges of fifty thousand square kilometers or less are confined. In this case, nine species match this definition: Chilean Woodstar, Coastal Miner, Thick-billed Miner, White-throated Earthcreeper, Surf Cinclodes, Cactus Canastero, Drab Seedeater, Slender-billed Finch, and Tamarugo Conebill. Three further species with slightly larger ranges—and hence not meeting the criteria as EBA trigger species—are mostly confined to this EBA: Streaked Tit-Spinetail, Pied-crested Tit-Tyrant, and Raimondi's Yellow-Finch. Important Bird Areas are now increasingly integrated with and referred to as Key Biodiversity Areas. Important Bird Areas in the region include Lomas de Lachay, Pantanos de Villa, Paracas National Park, Nazca, and Atiquipa. There are several official protected areas in this region, including Paracas National Park, which includes both terrestrial and marine areas, along with smaller reserves that conserve *lomas* and coastal marshes (such as those at Lomas de Lachay, and at Ventanilla, which lies on the coast immediately north of Lima).

In terms of globally threatened species, the region's most threatened bird is the Critically Endangered Chilean Woodstar, which is normally found only in and around the valley of Camarones in northern Chile, but has occasionally ranged farther north to Tacna, Peru. The species has suffered from habitat loss due to agricultural expansion in the few valleys where it was originally found and is also subject to hybridization with the much commoner and more widespread Peruvian Sheartail. The Endangered Black Rail is found in coastal marshes around Lima, and these could be threatened by development in the future. The Endangered Peruvian Tern nests in a few loose colonies in areas such as Paracas National Park, where it is subject to disturbance by all-terrain vehicles and dogs. Cat predation and coastal development also represent threats to this species.

Other Vulnerable species found in this area include the Chimney Swift, which winters in good numbers along the Peruvian coast, and the Humboldt Penguin, which breeds in rocky areas and on offshore islands. The little-known Peruvian Martin is also found here and is considered Near-Threatened. Several globally threatened seabirds also use offshore waters for foraging. These include the Critically Endangered Waved Albatross of the Galápagos Islands, as well as a few species that nest on the opposite side of the Pacific, such as the Chatham Albatross, Cook's Petrel, and Buller's Shearwater.

To address threats to birds in this area, emergency measures to rescue the Chilean Woodstar must continue, and protection for coastal marshes and Peruvian Tern nesting areas must be expanded. Andean Condors were once found around Paracas, and while they still visit the coast farther south—at the San Fernando National Reserve, for example—the reintroduction of condors to this area could be beneficial.

CACTUS CANASTERO (*Pseudasthenes cactorum*) is a highly restricted Peruvian endemic that can be found in appropriate habitat close to the coast of Lima and Arequipa Provinces and in the western foothills of Arequipa. It is strongly associated with columnar cacti and can skulk and be difficult to photograph. This picture was taken at Lomas de Asia, which is a good site for the species, although be ready for an uphill hike in the heat if you are there later in the day. COUNTRY ENDEMIC (PERU)

THE LAND OF THE NAZCA — BIRDING AND PHOTOGRAPHY SITES

The central Peruvian coast offers outstanding birding and photography opportunities. Primary among these are the Ballestas Islands off the coast of Paracas National Park, which offer the chance to see tens of thousands of seabirds at very close range. These include Guanay Cormorants, Peruvian Boobies, Red-legged Cormorants, Humboldt Penguins, Peruvian Pelicans, and Inca Terns. Back on land, Paracas National Park itself offers opportunities to see Chilean Flamingos, Snowy Plovers, Peruvian Terns, and groups of gulls that frequently include Gray Gulls and sometimes Andean Gulls from the highlands. Wintering species include Whimbrel, Surfbird, Royal and Elegant Terns, and large numbers of Franklin's Gulls.

A pelagic birding trip out of Lima is well worth the effort and can frequently yield close views of Cape Petrel, Ringed Storm-Petrel, Markham's Storm-Petrel, Waved Albatross, Peruvian Diving-Petrel, Sooty Shearwater, White-vented Storm-Petrel, and other tubenoses and pelagic seabirds. The sea here is cold and can be rough, so definitely prepare yourself for a big sea and, potentially, a smallish boat.

Coastal marshes such as those at Pantanos de Villa, Ventanilla, and El Paraíso offer the chance to find species such as White-tufted and Great Grebes, as well as Least Bittern, Cinnamon Teal, Amazilia Hummingbird, Plumbeous Rail, Slate-colored Coot, a good variety of wintering shorebirds, Puna Ibis, Long-tailed Mockingbird, and Peruvian Meadowlark. The popular reserve at Pantanos de Villa (immediately south of Lima) does not usually open until about 8:30 a.m., so be prepared to bird from the road prior to that. The road through the gated community next to the golf course to the southwest of the wetlands is normally open to visitors if you ask nicely. Once inside, you can scan the fields inland to the east, as well as the pool and beach at the end of the road. Look for Peruvian Thick-knees and Burrowing Owls on the open fields or even around the houses.

Another excellent area to check is Lomas de Lachay, which can be a good location to find Grayish Miner, Thick-billed Miner, Least Seedsnipe, and a range of other species typical of the foothills just inland from the coast. This site is about sixty miles north of Lima. Bear in mind that like other areas along the coast, the hills here can be shrouded in dense fog from about July to September, making birding, photography (especially), and even finding your way around somewhat challenging. Characteristic vegetation of the *lomas* includes species such as *Tara*, *Capparis*, and *Caesalpinia*.

No trip to the Lima coast would be complete without a visit to the more arid inland areas and oases, such as the scrub forest southwest of Las Antillas de Paracas (about five miles inland from Paracas), where Slender-billed Finch and Short-tailed Field-Tyrant can sometimes be found. The surrounding area is good for the endemic Coastal Miner, although this can also be seen on the ornamental lawns of the larger hotels in the town of Paracas. Another excellent location for birds such as the Cactus Canastero is Lomas de Asia, which lies about sixty miles south of Lima and a little inland of the Pan-American Highway. The canastero area requires an uphill walk with a round-trip of about four miles, so take plenty of water if you find yourself there in the heat of the day. The trees around the nearby Pueblo de Asia can also be worth a look for Oasis Hummingbird, and Peruvian Martins can potentially be found around the small nearby town (Pueblo de Asia).

Finally, the old Santa Eulalia Road—which has now been superseded as the main thoroughfare by the Central Highway, which crosses the Andes at Ticlio—is definitely worth a look. This is a classic narrow Andean mountain road along the edge of a deep gorge with no railing. The first section below the spectacular bridge across the gorge is excellent for birds typical of the western foothills—including the endemic Black-necked Woodpecker, which is usually found along the lower section of the road and is often associated with large columnar cacti. Farther up on a sharp bend before and below the bridge, Great Inca-Finch can sometimes be found. Peruvian Sheartails are common here, and Mountain Parakeets and even Andean Condor can sometimes be seen. The road eventually rejoins the Central Highway after passing Marcapomacocha and its now heavily harvested peat bogs. This boggy area sometimes also holds Diademed Sandpiper-Plover and, potentially, White-bellied Cinclodes.

ROYAL TERNS (*Thalasseus maximus*), front, and ELEGANT TERNS (*T. elegans*), rear, winter along the Peruvian coast. The differences in bill shape and color, and the different crown patterns—Elegant shows more black markings on the forecrown in non-breeding plumage—can easily be seen in this picture, which was taken at Paracas National Park, Peru.

COASTAL MINER (*Geositta peruviana*) is another Peruvian endemic that is found along the coastal plain from northern Peru to the south of Lima. These miners are often seen singly, or more often in pairs, running quickly across flat, dry areas between bushes. They can also be seen on the irrigated lawns of modern hotels in the town of Paracas. They are much paler than Common Miners, and there is no range overlap, as Common Miner is found farther south. COUNTRY ENDEMIC (PERU)

WEST PERUVIAN DOVE (*Zenaida meloda*) is often among the first species that birders arriving in Peru encounter. It is found from Ecuador to Chile (and even slightly into Argentina) and is abundant along the central coast of Peru, where it is the commonest dove in and around Lima, for example. Its abundance belies its subtle beauty, which is best appreciated with a close-up view.

ROYAL TERN (*Thalasseus maximus*) is a common nonbreeding visitor to this area. A collaboration between Virginia Tech and the U.S. Geological Survey Bird Banding Lab shows that most banded Royal Terns recorded along the Peruvian and Ecuadorian coasts nest in Virginia on the U.S. Atlantic coast. In 2019, a banded Royal Tern from the Hampton Roads area of Virginia was seen close to where this picture was taken.

WHITE-CHEEKED PINTAIL (*Anas bahamensis*) is an unmistakable small duck that is widespread in Latin America and the Caribbean. It is commonly found along the Peruvian and Ecuadorian coasts and less frequently into the Andean mountains themselves. It is common at the Villa wetlands, south of Lima, which is an especially good place to find this species and Cinnamon Teal.

GREATER YELLOWLEGS (*Tringa melanoleuca*) is a widespread and common nonbreeding species in the Andes and is frequently encountered along the Peruvian coast. It can be separated from the Lesser Yellowlegs by its thicker and longer (and slightly upturned) bill, larger size, and, often, its more penetrating three-note call. It nests in boreal Canada and southern Alaska.

BURROWING OWL (*Athene cunicularia*) is a widespread species that can be found along the Peruvian coast, in parts of the Andean highlands, and in Amazonia. These unique, small owls can often be seen during the day guarding the entrance to their nesting burrows, or right after the chicks have fledged but before they are ready to leave the safety of the nest, when family groups can sometimes be seen. Good sites for this species along the Peruvian coast include Lomas de Asia and Pantanos de Villa.

MANY-COLORED RUSH TYRANT (*Tachuris rubrigastra*) is one of the gems of the Peruvian coast and high-altitude lakes. Commonly found at sites such as the Villa and Ventanilla wetlands along the central Peruvian coast, this species is a must-see for most visitors. These incredibly beautiful and tiny tyrants are almost exclusively tied to giant totora sedges and often co-occur with the Wren-like Rushbird.

WREN-LIKE RUSHBIRD (*Phleocryptes melanops*) is commonly found alongside the Many-colored Rush Tyrant in large stands of totora sedges along the Peruvian coast and around high-altitude Andean lakes. The rushbird does skulk and can be hard to see in the dense vegetation but often flies between stands, making its squeaky and buzzy calls, and it may also reveal itself by uttering its ticking song.

RED-LEGGED CORMORANT (*Poikilocarbo gaimardi*) is a spectacular species (juvenile pictured). Found along the Peruvian coast, it then ranges south through Chile and along the coast of southern and eastern Argentina. Unlike the numerous Guanay Cormorants of the region, this species is most frequently found singly or in pairs among larger seabird colonies.

WHIMBREL (*Numenius phaeopus*) is a boreal migrant that nests in Alaska and northern Canada and winters along the coasts of South America. While the species is commonly found in the interior of the United States on migration, it hugs the shore when it reaches the South American continent. Whimbrels are abundant along the central coast of Peru, sometimes forming large roosting flocks—for example, on the beach close to the Villa wetlands, south of Lima.

CHILEAN FLAMINGO (*Phoenicopterus chilensis*) is the most widespread and easily encountered of the Andean flamingos. While it shares high-altitude lakes with both Andean and James's Flamingos, it is also found along the Peruvian coast at sites such as Paracas National Park—where flocks can often be seen in the southern part of the inlet immediately southwest of the town of Paracas. This is also the largest of the Andean flamingos, and a good field mark to distinguish Chilean Flamingos from other species of flamingo is their reddish knees, which contrast with their grayish legs.

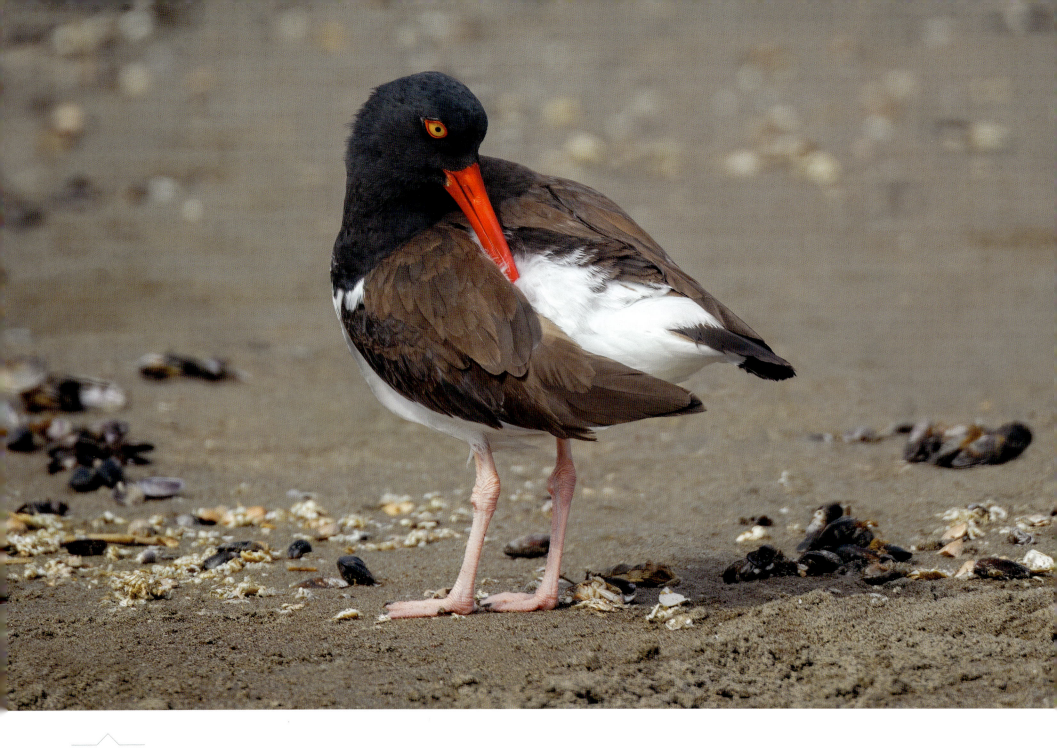

AMERICAN OYSTERCATCHER (*Haematopus palliatus*) is a loud, visible shorebird that is found along the coast, primarily on sandy beaches—unlike the Blackish Oystercatcher, which prefers rocky areas. American Oystercatchers are often encountered in pairs and can sometimes be found roosting in small groups. Their characteristic loud piping calls are often the first clue to their presence. They are widely distributed in coastal areas around the Americas, including along the Peruvian coast, where this photograph was taken.

SNOWY EGRET (*Egretta thula*) and the AMERICAN OYSTERCATCHER (*Haematopus palliatus*) can sometimes be found foraging together on beaches and tidal pools along the Peruvian coast south of Lima, where these birds were photographed.

SNOWY EGRET (*Egretta thula*) is a widespread species found in both coastal and Amazonian regions and occasionally on Andean lakes and pools. It can be recognized by its all-white plumage, bright yellow feet, and thin dark bill. The species sometimes also frequents coastal mudflats and tidal pools.

FRANKLIN'S GULL (*Leucophaeus pipixcan*) is a common nonbreeding visitor to the Peruvian coast. Franklin's Gulls nest on inland lakes and pools in the northern Great Plains of the United States and Canada. They can be confused with Laughing Gulls, which also winter along the Peruvian coast, but Franklin's Gulls have more white in their wing tips and more obvious white crescents around their eyes.

PERUVIAN THICK-KNEE (*Hesperoburhinus superciliaris*) is almost endemic to Peru but can also be found in parts of extreme northern Chile and along the Ecuadorian coast north to around Guayaquil. Like other thick-knees, the species is both crepuscular and nocturnal, and when encountered during the day, it is usually seen in pairs or small groups that are relatively inactive. They can be found along the coast in dry, open areas with small shrubs or in agricultural fields.

PERUVIAN PELICAN (*Pelecanus thagus*) is similar to—but larger than—the Brown Pelican, which also occurs along the northern and central Peruvian coast. The pale pattern on the wings and mantle of adult Peruvian Pelicans, most easily seen when the birds are in flight, is much more variegated than that of Brown Pelicans. Peruvian Pelicans can commonly be found in harbors along the coast, including around the town of Paracas and in the nearby national park.

The male **CINNAMON TEAL** (*Spatula cyanoptera*) is as distinctive as the female is nondescript. The status of this species in the Andes is complicated, since there are thought to be populations that migrate into the region from both the north (boreal migrants) and south (austral migrants) and there are also resident birds. The female can be confused with the female Blue-winged Teal but has a slightly longer bill, is warmer in color, and shows a subtly different face pattern. This species is easily found at sites such as the Pantanos de Villa wetlands, just south of Lima, Peru.

PERUVIAN BOOBY (*Sula variegata*) is another once very abundant species that has declined as a result of the historic collapse of the anchoveta shoals off the Peruvian coast. This seabird's northernmost breeding location is Isla Lobos de Tierra, and the species is generally replaced to the north of this colony by the Blue-footed Booby. Peruvian Boobies are very common off the Lima coast, and large numbers nest on the Ballestas Islands.

SURF CINCLODES (*Cinclodes taczanowskii*) is endemic to Peru and found only along the rocky shoreline of the central and southern coast. The seaweed-covered rocks around the small fishing village inside Paracas National Park are a reliable place to find these birds, although they can also be seen in Lima and at other rocky headland locations, including Pucusana.
COUNTRY ENDEMIC (PERU)

OASIS HUMMINGBIRD (*Rhodopis vesper*), a large hummingbird with an oversized-looking decurved bill, is found along the Peruvian coast and in mixed inland habitats at altitudes up to 10,000 feet or more. Oasis Hummingbirds are typically more difficult to find than other hummingbirds of the coastal zone, such as the Amazilia Hummingbird or Peruvian Sheartail, and one good place to look for them is in flowering trees in the vicinity of Pueblo de Asia, south of Lima.

BELCHER'S GULL (*Larus belcheri*) is an attractive and distinctive gull that is relatively common in Peru but rarely ventures north to Ecuador. The species nests on islands and on the mainland (but just at a few sites). It has a distinctive dark-headed nonbreeding plumage that makes it stand out from the similarly dark-backed Kelp Gulls, which are also often encountered in coastal ports and harbors.

HUMBOLDT PENGUIN (*Spheniscus humboldti*) is similar to the Magellanic Penguin, which is found farther south in Chile, but it has one black band across its chest, not two, and there are differences in its facial markings as well. Humboldt Penguins are uncommon and nest only in a few locations, including on the Ballestas Islands and at Pucusana, south of Lima. They are also sometimes encountered at sea, where they sit very low in the water and can be hard to keep track of as they dive among the waves.

BLACK-NECKED STILT (*Himantopus mexicanus*) breeds in wetlands along the Peruvian coast, including at Ventanilla, where these birds were photographed. Elsewhere, these elegant shorebirds are widely (though patchily) distributed in shallow wetlands and lagoons throughout the Americas. Two distinctive forms of the species are in the Andean region, and visitors should be on the lookout for the *melanurus* subspecies, which is found in the altiplano and in southern Amazonia. It has a white crown and hind collar.

THE COLOMBIAN ANDES | 2

IN COLOMBIA, THE Andes are divided into three cordilleras: the western (Cordillera Occidental), central (Cordillera Central), and eastern (Cordillera Oriental). The Western and Central Ranges are separated by the Cauca Valley to the north and by the Patía Valley to the south, and the Central and Eastern Ranges are separated by the Magdalena Valley. The Eastern Range extends into Venezuela along the Cordillera de Mérida and north through the mountains of the Serranía de Perijá. These ranges are topographically complex, and outlying extensions and valleys, such as the Serranía de los Yariguíes (which has an endemic brushfinch), lie to the west of the Eastern Cordillera about 130 miles north of Bogotá, while the dry Calima and Dagua Valleys extend west of the Western Cordillera. There is debate as to whether the Sierra Nevada de Santa Marta in northern Colombia is in fact an extension of the Andes.

While geologically the two ranges might be separate, the bird communities are very much connected, and hence we mention the area in this volume. While both the Cauca and Magdalena Valleys are to some degree independent centers of bird endemism, they also have a great deal in common, and are included together here along with the more northerly ranges. The western-facing slope of the Western Cordillera has much in common with the Chocó, which is treated separately in this book, and the eastern part of the Eastern Cordillera has much in common with the East Slope of the Andes overall, and this is covered under the East Slope chapter of this book. The páramos of the central Colombian Andes are also addressed in the páramo section. Some areas of the Colombian Andes are also covered in thorn scrub, similar to that found in Tumbesia and in parts of Ecuador to the north of Quito.

ANDEAN COCK-OF-THE-ROCK (*Rupicola peruvianus*) is one of the quintessential birds of the tropical Andes. The species is best known for its spectacular and noisy leks, at which multiple orange-red, black, and silver-gray males gather at dawn and dusk (and may remain close throughout the day) to attract a mate. The species affixes its nest to a rock face close to a river and feeds mostly on fruit. The birds are found at altitudes from about 1,500 feet to about 8,000 feet throughout the region.

THE COLOMBIAN ANDES — BIOGEOGRAPHY AND HISTORY

A significant component of the Colombian Andes lies within the Cauca and Magdalena Valleys, and these are two of the main destinations for birding in the region. These valleys have a lot in common with each other both biogeographically and ornithologically, although each has its own endemic birds. Both valleys have a variety of drier forest and scrub at lower elevations and humid evergreen Andean Cloud Forest at higher elevations. While the upper slopes have certainly lost a significant amount of forest to agriculture, the dry forest in the lower reaches of the valleys closer to the rivers is even more degraded and threatened. Above the cloud forest on higher slopes, it is possible to find areas of Cushion Páramo as well as some elfin and *Polylepis* forests that have their own bird assemblages. (Elfin forest is characterized by stunted, gnarled trees with abundant lichens and thick moss ground cover.) Toward the northern end of both valleys, an area of humid tropical lowland forest has some commonalities with the Chocó and is sometimes referred to as the Nechí Lowlands.

The Colombian central Andes are not especially high in elevation when compared with those in Ecuador, Peru, and Bolivia; they have a main ridgeline at about 10,000 feet, with occasional higher peaks or massifs, such as Nevados del Huila, Ruiz, del Cumbal, Tolima, and Chiles, as well as Volcán Puracé. Two other major areas of bird endemism in northern Colombia not covered elsewhere in this book are the Serranía de Perijá and the Sierra Nevada de Santa Marta. Due to its remoteness and security concerns over recent decades, the Serranía de Perijá is still relatively poorly known ornithologically, although this has begun to change in recent years. It has at least six endemic bird species and additional subspecies that may be split over time. The Santa Marta area is much better studied and birded and has a dedicated birding lodge at El Dorado run by Fundación ProAves. The Santa Marta Range is an isolated granite massif that includes one of the two equal highest peaks in Colombia, Pico Cristóbal Colón, at just under 19,000 feet. It is geologically separate from the Andes but remains connected through its avifauna.

This huge region is culturally complex and, unlike much of the Andes to the south, was never conquered by the Incas. Prior to Spanish colonization, several indigenous groups held significant influence in the region, including the Kogi, Muisca, Quimbaya, and Tairona. Spanish colonization began in 1492, and in 1819, following more than three centuries of Spanish rule, Colombia became independent from Spain as part of Gran Colombia—an earlier larger grouping of what are now several independent South American nations. Panama and Colombia then split from this group of nations, with the two countries themselves separating from each other in 1903 to create the present-day configuration of nations.

BIRD DIVERSITY AND SPECIALTIES — THE COLOMBIAN ANDES

Colombia is the nation with the most bird species, with a current list of 1,958. The country also has close to one hundred endemic species and, with forthcoming splits, may well pass this number in the near future. This list of country endemics (species found only within the national borders of a single country) includes such iconic species as the Bogotá Rail, Black Inca, Dusky Starfrontlet, Yellow-eared Parrot, Cundinamarca Antpitta, Red-bellied Grackle, Gold-ringed Tanager, and Multicolored Tanager. A large majority of these endemics are found within the central and northern Andes region. Fortunately, Colombia has an excellent field guide in Steven Hilty and William Brown's *A Guide to the Birds of Colombia*, also published by Princeton University Press, which documents the country's amazing avian diversity in a way that is not possible in this volume. Other good books on Colombian birds include *An Illustrated Field Guide to the Birds of Colombia* by Fernando Ayerbe Quiñones, as well as a similarly titled work by Miles McMullan and a newer volume by Hilty. So plenty of choice and lots of good bird information are available to the prospective visitor.

BUFF-WINGED STARFRONTLET (*Coeligena lutetiae*) is a stunning, large hummingbird of the highlands. The pale buffy patch on the inner secondaries is unique to this distinctive species (female pictured). It is found in cloud and elfin forest of the central Andes south to northern Peru and at altitudes of about 9,000 feet and above.

97

THE COLOMBIAN ANDES › CONSERVATION

Like many developing countries, Colombia has experienced significant deforestation, especially in the fertile inter-Andean valleys and lowlands. Despite this, the country has an excellent system of protected areas, with 1,330 official protected areas covering 16.4 percent of the country's area. Colombia has 10 Endemic Bird Areas, 86 globally threatened bird species, 128 Important Bird Areas, and 42 Alliance for Zero Extinction Sites (a location with at least one globally Endangered or Critically Endangered species confined to it). Colombia also has thirty-eight bird species that BirdLife International considers either Endangered or Critically Endangered. These include such emblematic species as the Blue-billed Curassow, Blue-bearded Helmetcrest, Gorgeted Puffleg, Banded Ground-Cuckoo, Great Green Macaw, Recurve-billed Bushbird, Chestnut-capped Piha, Santa Marta Sabrewing, Red Siskin, Mountain Grackle, and Apolinar's Wren.

Colombia has several effective bird and wildlife conservation groups, including the governmental Alexander von Humboldt Biological Resources Research Institute and Asociación Calidris, which is a nongovernmental organization and BirdLife partner dedicated to bird conservation. Fundación ProAves is the primary partner of American Bird Conservancy in Colombia. Originally founded to prevent the extinction of the threatened Yellow-eared Parrot, ProAves then expanded to set up additional bird reserves across the country, and is currently operating twenty-eight such protected areas in many of the most critical sites for threatened birds. American Bird Conservancy has been actively supporting bird conservation in Colombia, including land acquisition and reserve creation and sustainability, for over twenty years, especially in partnership with ProAves. American Bird Conservancy's work in Colombia has also expanded recently to include such partners as Fundación Biodiversa Colombia, Fundación Camaná Conservación y Territorio, Fundación Ecohabitats, Corporación SalvaMontes, and Fundación Guanacas, among others, to conserve species such as the Antioquia Brushfinch, Blue-billed Curassow, Cundinamarca Antpitta, and Gorgeted Puffleg. Colombia has a national bird conservation strategy, a growing birding and ornithology community, and even a YouTube channel—The Birder's Show—dedicated to birds and conservation.

TRICOLORED BRUSHFINCH (*Atlapetes tricolor*) is an interesting species in that it is found primarily on the western slopes of Colombia and Ecuador at altitudes up to about 6,500 feet, but in Peru, it flips its distribution to the East Slope. These brushfinches tend to skulk a bit less than others—and while they are similar in appearance to, for example, Pale-naped and Rufous-capped Brushfinches, they occupy different ranges and altitudes and have unique plumage characteristics (such as the lack of a white wing spot) that distinguish them.

BIRDING AND PHOTOGRAPHY SITES — THE COLOMBIAN ANDES

This region is undoubtedly one of the greatest birding areas on Earth. Until recently, Colombia was considered to be off-limits to birders due to security concerns, and indeed one group of birders from New York was kidnapped by rebels in 1998, although all were eventually released (or escaped) unharmed. In 2016, the Colombian government signed a peace agreement with the leftist rebel group known as the Revolutionary Armed Forces of Colombia (FARC), bringing an end to decades of armed conflict in the country. Since then, birding tourism has taken off significantly. There is an excellent network of bird reserves and lodges, many of which have feeders that can be very attractive to photographers seeking close-up shots of hummingbirds and tanagers. Fundación ProAves operates twenty-eight bird reserves throughout Colombia, and several have excellent lodges for birders. Details can be found at proaves.org. Note that it is very important to book in advance. There are many other great lodges and facilities for birders, including, for example, La Minga, Araucana Lodge, and Finca Alejandría in the Cauca Valley; Montezuma Road Ecolodge in Tatama National Park; the Hummingbird Observatory near Bogotá; Rancho Camaná, which is a good base to visit the Cundinamarca Antpitta site; the Enchanted Garden near Tabacal; and many more.

SCRUB TANAGER (*Stilpnia vitriolina*) is found in mid-elevational habitats of western Colombia and northwestern Ecuador. It is most often recorded in open scrubby and secondary habitats and is commonly seen close to settled areas. This species is typically found where mixed-species flocks are uncommon and, instead, occurs alone or in pairs, foraging for insects and fruit.

ANDEAN GUAN (*Penelope montagnii*) is found from Venezuela in the north to Bolivia in the south, truly spanning the full range of the tropical Andes. It is a typical guan, which means it can skulk, but it can also be seen conspicuously and clumsily climbing around in trees searching for the fruits that are its primary food.

CROWNED WOODNYMPH (*Thalurania colombica*) is widespread from Belize to Ecuador (female pictured). There is a confusing array of potential subspecies and forms with complicated mixtures of morphology—especially in Colombia—where some populations have violet-crowned males, and others have green-crowned males. Violet-crowned birds tend to predominate in the northern part of the species range, however.

CINNAMON FLYCATCHER (*Pyrrhomyias cinnamomeus*) is primarily a bird of the cloud forest and is often first noticed due to its familiar, sputtering, trill-like call. The species is found at altitudes up to about 9,000 feet. Its global distribution aligns very closely with the high Andean mountain chain, spanning from Venezuela to Chile.

WHITE-TIPPED QUETZAL (*Pharomachrus fulgidus*) has a very limited range in northern Colombia and nearby Venezuela. It is similar in appearance to the widespread Crested Quetzal, but the two species do not overlap in range. Unlike the Resplendent Quetzal of Central America, South American quetzals do not have especially long tails, but their habits are otherwise similar—feeding on insects and fruit and nesting in tree cavities.

SANTA MARTA BRUSHFINCH (*Atlapetes melanocephalus*) is an attractive and distinctive brushfinch that is often the first Santa Marta endemic encountered by visitors. It is found in cloud forest and clearings at altitudes up to 10,000 feet and commonly occurs in small groups of up to six or more birds. **COUNTRY ENDEMIC (COLOMBIA)**

AMAZON KINGFISHER (*Chloroceryle amazona*) is the second largest resident South American kingfisher, after the Ringed. It looks like an oversized Green Kingfisher but lacks the conspicuous white spots on the wings and has one, not two, breast bands. While it is common throughout Amazonia, it is by no means confined to that region and is also found throughout Colombia's major valleys, reaching as far north as South Texas as a vagrant.

TYRANNINE WOODCREEPER (*Dendrocincla tyrannina*) is found at altitudes from 4,500 feet to about 10,000 feet on both slopes, and ranges from Colombia to Bolivia. It tends to be uncommon and solitary and typically keeps to the mid-story of the forest. This species is one of the more readily identifiable woodcreepers, with its unstreaked plumage and long, dark, and slightly hook-tipped bill.

SOUTHERN EMERALD-TOUCANET (*Aulacorhynchus albivitta*) is a striking and charismatic species found in a variety of forested and secondary habitats at altitudes up to about 10,000 feet. It is widespread in the Colombian Andes, but in Ecuador and Peru it is primarily a bird of the East Slope. Toucanets are omnivorous, and while insects and fruits probably make up the bulk of their diet, they will also eat lizards, and the eggs and nestlings of other birds.

WHITE-NECKED JACOBIN (*Florisuga mellivora*) is a striking hummingbird that is widespread at lower elevations throughout the Andes and across Amazonia, ranging north as far as Mexico. Like some other hummingbirds, the females are less colorful and can present an identification challenge until you become familiar with them.

CARIB GRACKLE (*Quiscalus lugubris*) is a common but local bird of the Colombian eastern Andes and lowlands, found at altitudes up to about 2,000 feet. These gregarious birds are typical noisy, boisterous grackles. They are often found in developed areas and can nest and gather in large groups. The species is also found in Panama, the Caribbean, and northeastern Brazil. The Carib Grackle is smaller than the similar Great-tailed Grackle, which is confined mainly to more western parts of Colombia.

LITTLE TINAMOU (*Crypturellus soui*) is a lowland species that is widespread in Colombia and Ecuador, but as it ranges south through Peru, its distribution becomes closely tied to the East Slope and the Amazonian ecosystem. Like most forest tinamous, this species is best located by call. This is one of relatively few bird species in which the female is more brightly colored than the male, and it is also the male that incubates the eggs (as in other tinamous).

BROWN VIOLETEAR (*Colibri delphinae*) is, at first glance, one of the dullest of the cloud forest hummingbirds. However, like many other hummingbird species, it hides a secret that becomes obvious only when viewed from a certain angle—when light both reflects from and refracts through its feather structures. When this happens, the bird displays iridescent purple ear coverts and a shimmering green throat patch sometimes edged below by blue. Hummingbird colors are likely even more amazing to the hummingbirds themselves, because their ability to detect ultraviolet light is much better than ours. The species is widespread throughout the Andes south to Bolivia at altitudes up to about 8,500 feet.

CATTLE TYRANT (*Machetornis rixosa*) has a disjunct range, with one population in northern South America and another found from Brazil to Argentina. Cattle Tyrants can resemble a Western or Tropical Kingbird but are typically found walking on their long legs or even perched on a cow or other grazing animal. They feed on insects attracted to or disturbed by cattle and other animals.

STRIPED TREEHUNTER (*Thripadectes holostictus*) is one of several similar-looking treehunters that can be found in the Andes. Distribution and altitude can be important clues to identification when individual birds are not seen especially well, which is often the case with these furtive birds, which tend to lurk around the base of mossy trees or forage among bromeliads close to the ground or in the mid-story. This species is found patchily from Venezuela to northern Bolivia at altitudes up to about 9,000 feet.

SNAIL KITE (*Rostrhamus sociabilis*) is a widespread neotropical raptor that is found almost throughout the lowlands of Colombia and Ecuador (female pictured); but elsewhere in South America, it tends to be more strongly linked to Amazonian habitats than to those in the Andes. This species has a strongly hooked bill designed to remove its favored prey, the apple snail, from its shell. Snail Kites are almost exclusively associated with wetlands, including marshy lakes or rice paddies. When seen in flight, their strongly rounded wings are a good clue to their identity.

COLOMBIAN CHACHALACA (*Ortalis columbiana*) is found in central Colombia on slopes above both the Cauca and Magdalena Valleys. It was recently split from Speckled Chachalaca based on plumage and vocal differences. These chachalacas are similar in appearance to Guans of the genus *Penelope*. COUNTRY ENDEMIC (COLOMBIA)

SIERRA NEVADA BRUSHFINCH (*Arremon basilicus*) was split from the Stripe-headed Brushfinch as recently as 2010. The two species are generally similar in appearance, but the Sierra Nevada Brushfinch has a black crescent on its breast and has different vocalizations. Typically a skulker, it has an extremely limited range in northern Colombia but can be seen at the feeders at ProAves's El Dorado Reserve. COUNTRY ENDEMIC (COLOMBIA)

SOCIAL FLYCATCHER (*Myiozetetes similis*) is a common and widespread species in open and secondary habitats, and it shares many plumage characteristics with several other common neotropical species, such as the Great Kiskadee and Rusty-margined Flycatcher. Aids to identifying this species are its call notes, small bill, and plain brown wings. Social Flycatchers are widely distributed in Colombia and Ecuador, and elsewhere tend to be found on the East Slope, in the eastern foothills, and in Amazonia.

BLUE-WINGED MOUNTAIN TANAGER (*Anisognathus somptuosus*) is one of the most striking common residents of mid- to upper-elevation cloud forest. These colorful birds are widespread in central and southern Colombia and are also seen easily at such locations as Paz de las Aves and Bellavista Lodge, in Ecuador; and near Abra Patricia, in Peru. This species is found on both eastern and western Andean slopes from Venezuela to Bolivia and normally occurs at elevations up to 8,500 feet.

WHITE-HEADED MARSH TYRANT (*Arundinicola leucocephala*) is a widespread and common species in the lowlands. Males are more or less unmistakable, with their black body and white head. Females resemble other water-tyrants but can be separated by studying plumage features with care. These attractive and appealing birds are often seen perched over water, flicking their tails and flycatching.

PIED WATER-TYRANT (*Fluvicola pica*) can be found around wetlands in the lowlands of northern South America. These birds are often easily seen as they forage over or around water, flicking their tails and calling. Their ball-like nests are usually built low over water.

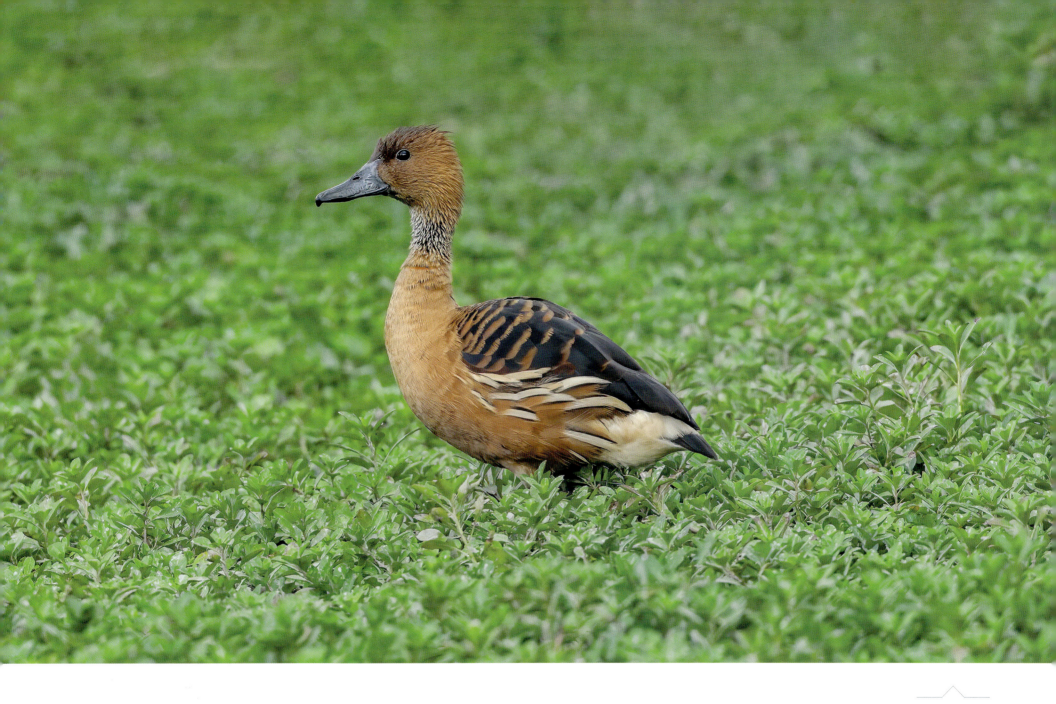

FULVOUS WHISTLING-DUCK (*Dendrocygna bicolor*) is a widespread neotropical species found in wetlands in the Cauca and Magdalena Valleys of Colombia, extending patchily south to Bolivia and Argentina and north to the southern United States. Like the White-faced Whistling-Duck, this species is also found outside the Americas and occurs in both Africa and Asia.

DUSKY CHLOROSPINGUS (*Chlorospingus semifuscus*) was once considered to be a tanager (Dusky, or Dusky-bellied Bush Tanager), but recent studies have recognized that it is in fact more closely related to sparrows—such as the Olive Sparrow of North America. The Dusky Chlorospingus is fairly common throughout its narrow range from Colombia to Ecuador, where it can be found in cloud forest at altitudes up to about 8,000 feet.

BUFF-TAILED CORONET (*Boissonneaua flavescens*) is widespread throughout the Colombian and Ecuadorian Andes, extending northeast into Venezuela along the Cordillera de Mérida. The species is considered to be of Least Concern from a conservation standpoint due to its large range. It inhabits cloud forest from about 5,000 to 8,000 feet in altitude.

CARIBBEAN HORNERO

(*Furnarius longirostris*) is found in the northern lowlands and Andean valleys of Colombia south to approximately Cali. Horneros are real characters of the bird world, making themselves obvious with their loud calls or by sitting atop their dome-shaped mud nests. *Hornero* is Spanish for "oven" and refers to the oven-like nests made by the birds. Horneros can frequently be seen walking on the ground or across roads in developed areas, although some members of the genus also have somewhat more specific natural habitat preferences (such as Várzea Forest in the case of Pale-legged Hornero, for example).

RUSSET-CROWNED WARBLER (*Myiothlypis coronata*) is a bird of the Andean cloud forests and is found at altitudes up to about 10,000 feet, where it gleans insects and other food items from tree trunks and from vegetation close to the ground. It is found from Venezuela to Bolivia and, while not uncommon, can skulk and is not always easy to see well.

COMMON POTOO (*Nyctibius griseus*), like other potoos, is most frequently seen imitating a branch at a known roosting location. These birds can be incredibly hard to spot due to their excellent camouflage and are one of the least distinctively marked of the potoos. They are found widely throughout the neotropics, and populations in Mexico and the Caribbean may hold one or more additional cryptic (nonobvious and undescribed) species. On moonlit nights, the species is most readily detected by its song, which is a distinctive series of mournful, descending whistles.

BAND-TAILED GUAN (*Penelope argyrotis*) is found in humid forest from northwestern Venezuela to northeastern Colombia—including in the Santa Marta Mountains—from 3,000 to 7,500 feet in altitude. These guans are mostly arboreal but may visit the ground on occasion to forage on fallen fruits. The tail band is not easily seen, but the species is found at lower altitudes than the similar Andean Guan, aiding with separation of the species. The Santa Marta Range is one of, if not *the* best and most accessible places to find this species.

BLACK-BILLED THRUSH (*Turdus ignobilis*) is a widespread species found throughout the Colombian Andes and lowlands. It is frequently seen in urban areas and is the robin of Colombia in many ways. The species is drab overall and sings a typical thrush-like song. It has two subspecies that vary mostly in throat pattern; birds in the eastern portion of the species' range have a whiter throat.

SPECTACLED PARROTLET
(*Forpus conspicillatus*) is a tiny, cute parrot that is mostly confined to Colombia, where it is widespread in the north and west. Females are all green, but the males have blue in the face and wings. These parrotlets are frequently found in flocks in open habitats and agricultural areas.

ORANGE-BELLIED EUPHONIA (*Euphonia xanthogaster*) is another widespread member of this genus, best separated from the Thick-billed Euphonia (the other common, widespread euphonia) by its dark throat. Other euphonias look similar, though, and are best separated based on range and other plumage details (e.g., crown pattern and throat and overall color). Euphonias are related to finches and are familiar Andean birds, often seen accompanying mixed flocks or attending feeders. They build ball-like mossy nests and are known to be an important disperser of mistletoe seeds, and these can sometimes be seen in strands of their droppings left clinging to twigs and small branches.

GLOSSY FLOWERPIERCER (*Diglossa lafresnayii*) is found from Colombia to northern Peru at altitudes up to and slightly above 12,000 feet. Glossy and Black Flowerpiercers can be difficult to separate in the field in the eastern Andes of Colombia, where the two species share the pale shoulder patch—although this patch is smaller and duller in the Black Flowerpiercer, and Black also favors drier habitats, which can be another clue to its identity. In most areas, though, the pale shoulder patch of Glossy is distinctive. While hummingbirds probe flowers for nectar, flowerpiercers "cheat", accessing the nectar by nipping the flowers close to the base with their sharp, hooked bills.

GOLDEN-BELLIED FLYCATCHER (*Myiodynastes hemichrysus*) is superficially similar in appearance to the group of flycatchers that includes the kiskadees and Social Flycatcher. Golden-bellied, however, shows a dark moustachial stripe framing the pale lower ear coverts. The stripe is lacking in other similar species. The Golden-bellied Flycatcher is found from Venezuela to Ecuador and was recently split from the Golden-crowned Flycatcher of Peru and Bolivia based on its call and additional minor morphological differences.

The aptly named SQUIRREL CUCKOO (*Piaya cayana*) is widespread in forest and second growth throughout the neotropics. It can be found in both arid and moist habitats hopping through the branches of trees, at times resembling a squirrel. The long tail is probably the most distinctive feature of the species, which can often be identified by shape alone. While these birds are widespread and common, they frequently seem to melt into trees or brush on landing so that unobstructed views for good photographs are difficult to come by.

BLACK-STRIPED SPARROW (*Arremonops conirostris*) is a widespread and unobtrusive species that is often seen feeding on the ground or in low shrubs. It is primarily a bird of the lowlands but can be found at altitudes up to 5,000 feet or more in places. It is usually found alone or in pairs. Its distinctive song is often the best clue to its presence.

BARRED ANTSHRIKE (*Thamnophilus doliatus*) is found in northern Colombia and the Magdalena Valley. It also ranges south to Peru and Bolivia. The striking males are similar to Lined Antshrikes, but the barring is less dense, so the bird appears lighter overall. Lined Antshrikes also mostly have different geographic and altitudinal ranges. The similar Bar-crested Antshrike replaces Barred in the Cauca Valley of Colombia and generally also at higher elevations elsewhere. Some antshrikes are best identified based on the more distinctive female plumage, since the birds are often seen in pairs. Barred Antshrikes are usually found in dense, scrubby habitats and in the understory, where they can be hard to see well.

ANDEAN EMERALD (*Uranomitra franciae*) is a small, attractive hummingbird found from Colombia to Peru. It occurs from mid-elevations to about 9,000 feet in altitude and its snow-white underparts are a good clue to its identity. It is frequently found in more open habitats close to forest and is often seen at feeders.

GOLDEN-BREASTED PUFFLEG (*Eriocnemis mosquera*) is found in Colombia and northern Ecuador at altitudes reaching 11,000 feet or more. This elegant, large puffleg has a forked tail, and the "golden breast" seems more like a collar extending around the sides of the neck. It is a bird of the forest and forest edge and visits feeders in some areas, including at the Zuroloma and Yanacocha Reserves, in northwestern Ecuador.

SCALED DOVE (*Columbina squammata*) is another species with a disjunct range—interestingly, approximately mirroring that of the Cattle Tyrant—with separate populations in both northern and southeastern South America. This delicate-looking species, with its intricate black feather edgings, lights up with rufous as it shows its primaries in flight. It is commonly found in open habitats and developed areas.

GOLDEN-NAPED TANAGER (*Chalcothraupis ruficervix*) ranges from Colombia to Bolivia. It is most widespread in Colombia, and while it occurs on both slopes in Ecuador, it is an East Slope bird in Peru. It is found in humid forest at low to mid-elevations and often feeds in or close to the canopy on fruits and berries, especially on shrubs of the genus *Miconia*. These tanagers sometimes also attend fruit feeders—where they can be photographed more easily than in their usual arboreal foraging zone.

CHESTNUT-HEADED OROPENDOLA (*Psarocolius wagleri*) ranges from Central America to Ecuador and is found in second-growth and forest-edge habitats in the lowlands. Like other oropendolas, Chestnut-headed Oropendolas build large basket-like nests that hang in groups from trees. The birds are most often seen in the canopy feeding on fruits, or during flights between trees, when their yellow outer tail feathers can be obvious. From a distance, they can be mistaken for Crested Oropendolas, but Chestnut-headeds are much smaller.

RUSSET-THROATED PUFFBIRD (*Hypnelus ruficollis*) is confined to northern Colombia and adjacent parts of Venezuela and Panama. It is found in dry, deciduous forest and scrub at altitudes up to about 4,000 feet, where it is the only puffbird present. This is the "best of both worlds" puffbird, in that it has both a black breast band and a rufous throat—most other Colombian puffbirds have either one or the other. This species of puffbird also tends to be more gregarious than most and will nest in a termite or abandoned hornero nest.

BLACK-CAPPED TANAGER (*Stilpnia heinei*) is found from Santa Marta through western Colombia and Ecuador into northern Peru. The species is one of the less common tanagers in its range and is usually found in pairs in second growth and scrub at altitudes up to about 9,000 feet. On first glance, the males can be reminiscent of Beryl-spangled Tanagers, but the black cap of this species is diagnostic.

MONTANE WOODCREEPER (*Lepidocolaptes lacrymiger*) is one of a number of potentially confusing birds that are often best photographed to confirm their identities. Other clues are altitudinal range and distribution, but this bird is often seen only briefly before it hops behind a trunk or limb (to which it habitually clings). This species is found on both slopes at altitudes from about 5,000 to 10,000 feet in humid montane forest.

FROM THE FIELD — *Personal stories from the leaders of American Bird Conservancy's primary bird and habitat conservation partners in the tropical Andes.*

THE THREAT OF EXTINCTION SPARKS A NEW BIRD CONSERVATION MOVEMENT IN COLOMBIA

MOST RECENTLY, THE sea and land have suffered deep, irreparable environmental wounds in their ecosystems, such as water and soil pollution, deforestation, extinction of species, and biodiversity loss, destroying Mother Earth. The most painful thing is that these wounds are the result of unconscious self-injury caused, ironically, by human activity—and what are we humans but a species of nature? With this honest reflection, I want to introduce myself. I am Sara Inés Lara, a woman passionate about conservation who is proud to be an indigenous person from the Andes of southern Colombia.

I grew up in a small rural town called Cajibío, located in the Cauca Department in the Colombian high Andes, a world treasure of biodiversity and natural resources but also a territory devastated by decades of conflict, where the losses to people and nature are incalculable. I was educated as a civil engineer at a time when little was said about the conservation and protection of birds, clearly a topic for only a few; for me, growing up in the mountains surrounded by beauty and apparent abundance, it was not obvious to know and understand that many species were disappearing.

Luckily, I had the opportunity to learn about the reality of many unique and threatened species, such as the Yellow-eared Parrot, the Blue-billed Curassow, and dozens of beautiful hummingbird species, some even discovered in recent years and carrying a sentence of imminent extinction.

In 2002, I decided to change course in my life, leaving Haliburton and my thriving engineering career to become part of Fundación ProAves, the recently hatched Colombian nongovernmental conservation organization. From this point forward, I embarked on and dedicated my life to the conservation of birds and their habitats in my beautiful country and its remote territories.

It has been a tremendous challenge, especially with the significant pressures in many forms; however, during my career, I have managed to lead and mobilize strategic conservation processes for the benefit of nature and threatened bird species. This has included habitat conservation through the establishment of the largest network of private bird reserves in the tropics, with twenty-eight reserves, protecting over 12 percent of all bird species on Earth, in addition to saving critical sites for migratory species received each nonbreeding season. This network has become a beacon of hope for species recovery and a catalyst for local communities to invest in greener alternatives, such as ecotourism and bird tourism, contributing to greatly improved local livelihoods.

For over two decades in conservation, it has become apparent that gender and youth inclusion are critical pillars to ensuring a profound change of consciousness planted deeply in the roots and fundamentals of our society. Recognizing that nature and all species play a vital part in preserving the human realm, I have always fought to create opportunities for gender and minority inclusion in rural and less advantaged communities.

I invite you to visit Colombia to enjoy spectacular places dedicated to protecting the rich birdlife in the reserves created by ProAves, thanks to the support of individuals and institutions such as American Bird Conservancy, which believes in the power of empowering communities through the establishment of initiatives designed and implemented by those who are on the front line of conservation.

I am a living example and testimony to the importance of environmental education. Thanks to the knowledge once shared with me, I have become an activist in the world of bird conservation, and my story will encourage others to see that each of us has a role to play and actions to take.

We must continue to send a clear message about the urgency of repairing the damage we have caused to Mother Nature. Let us all change the course of destruction, pollution, and species loss in countries with both high and lower biodiversity.

SARA INÉS LARA
Executive Director, Fundación ProAves
Founder and President, Women for Conservation

BUFF-TAILED CORONET (*Boissonneaua flavescens*) is a feisty, medium-sized hummingbird that occurs widely across the western slope of Ecuador and Colombia, and also reaches into western Venezuela. They are commonly seen at feeders, and a great place to find them is at ProAves Colombia's Las Tángaras Reserve, which lies around 90 miles southwest of Medellín. The reserve has a total bird list of 565 species, including 13 endemics.

THE HIGH ANDES 3

THE HIGH ANDES must be one of the greatest birding areas on the planet. It is both incredibly varied and absolutely unique in its landscape, culture, avifauna, and overall biodiversity. This is the land that was once the realm of the great Incan Empire. Its control has shifted multiple times, and yet it still retains much of its traditional culture, and the Incan language of Quechua is still widely spoken. This is the territory of the Andean Condor, the Giant Hummingbird, and three species of spectacular flamingo that scrape out a living on lakes that lie almost at the roof of the world. Any birding trip from sea level to this region presupposes that acclimatization for at least a couple of nights will be needed before undertaking any strenuous hiking. The birds of the region are very well represented in the classic book *Birds of the High Andes* by Jon Fjeldså and Niels Krabbe. While this book has somewhat been superseded by more recent national field guides and birding apps, it is still very well worth buying. The illustrations are superb, and it somehow catches the feeling of high-altitude birding better than any other field guide.

JAMES'S FLAMINGO (*Phoenicoparrus jamesi*) is one of three flamingo species that gather to breed at Laguna Hedionda in the Bolivian highlands. Shallow, high-altitude lakes like this (including in Argentina and Chile) hold the entire global breeding population of this strikingly beautiful species.

ANDEAN GULL (*Chroicocephalus serranus*) is the only gull species regularly found in the high Andes. These attractive birds are often seen around high-altitude lakes, and they nest colonially at altitudes up to 14,500 feet. They are commonly seen in groups on the lake below Jocotoco's Chakana Reserve in Ecuador and in the nearby Antisana Ecological Reserve. In winter, they lack the black head (which is replaced by a dark ear spot) and may occasionally be found along the coast.

BIOGEOGRAPHY AND HISTORY — THE PÁRAMO

The páramo is sandwiched between the high peaks of the Andes and the upper edge of the cloud forest. It is comprised of humid bunch and tussock grassland (for example, *Calamagrostis* and *Festuca*) often mixed with boggy areas, with *Polylepis* forest, and sometimes with areas of dry or humid puna-like grassland, as well as various low-lying shrubs, cushion plants, and *Espeletias* (sometimes described as Cushion Páramo or Grassy Páramo). In northern areas, emergent rosette-forming plants known as *frailejones* are commonly found among the tussock and other grasses. Páramo is found throughout the northern Andes, generally above 10,000 feet, and the most extensive areas are found in the highlands of Colombia and Ecuador and somewhat into Venezuela. It tends to be replaced by drier puna south of the Marañón River in northern Peru. One quintessential bird of the páramo is the Tawny Antpitta. It is perhaps the easiest species of its genus to see, partly because its habitat is open (other antpittas are mainly in cloud forest or denser habitats), and perhaps because it also seems a bit less shy. It is the squeaky three-note call of the Tawny Antpitta that often defines the birding experience in the páramo. Páramo is also defined by altitude and humidity. It is slow growing and, once disturbed, can take a very long period to recover. In the lower-elevation páramos, soils tend to be acidic and comprised mainly of organic material, rather than being derived from the weathering of the underlying substrate, whereas at higher elevations, organic accretion is limited and soils tend to be sandier and more linked to the bedrock in their composition. While rainfall isn't necessarily especially high, the frequent mists and fog ensure that these habitats remain extremely humid.

Much of the southern páramo was once included in territory under Incan rule, although the Incas failed to conquer the Colombian Andes, which remained under the control of cultures such as the Nariño, Tolima, and Muisca. Due to the cold, wet, and less-fertile nature of higher-elevation páramo, it has often been spared the more serious impacts of human development that have affected lower slopes, although burning, grazing, agriculture, and mining still remain threats. There is debate concerning the extent to which páramo is a human-adapted system that historically depended on fire, but despite evidence of early agriculture, it seems that pre-Columbian cultures considered páramos primarily sacred and used them for hunting or for burying the dead. In Ecuador, páramo areas were historically available for the public to graze cattle, and burning and cattle grazing likely had significant impacts on natural habitats. However, following the development of agrarian reform policies, this has been changing, and indigenous communities have been regaining rights to manage some of these lands, although agriculture has also been pushed upslope as well—so there have been mixed outcomes for páramo conservation. There is also an increasing recognition that large Andean cities, such as Quito and Bogotá, depend on páramos to provide a consistent water supply, and this will hopefully play a role in ensuring their future protection.

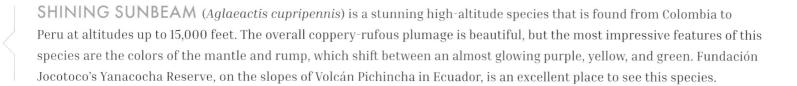

SHINING SUNBEAM (*Aglaeactis cupripennis*) is a stunning high-altitude species that is found from Colombia to Peru at altitudes up to 15,000 feet. The overall coppery-rufous plumage is beautiful, but the most impressive features of this species are the colors of the mantle and rump, which shift between an almost glowing purple, yellow, and green. Fundación Jocotoco's Yanacocha Reserve, on the slopes of Volcán Pichincha in Ecuador, is an excellent place to see this species.

THE PÁRAMO > BIRD DIVERSITY AND SPECIALTIES

This high-elevation, high-humidity life zone does not have the highest diversity of bird species in the Andes by any means, but the birds that are found here are often restricted to this habitat, and they still represent a key element of the high Andean avifauna. Species that can be encountered, depending on location, include the aforementioned Tawny Antpitta, Andean Condor, Carunculated Caracara, Ecuadorian and Blue-throated Hillstars (especially in the vicinity of *Chuquiraga* flowers), Blue-bearded Helmetcrest, Andean Ibis, Andean Gull, Rufous-bellied Seedsnipe, Stout-billed Cinclodes, Black-winged Ground Dove, and Rainbow-bearded Thornbill, as well as shrike-tyrants, canasteros, spinetails, chat-tyrants, and many other species.

ANDEAN IBIS (*Theristicus branickii*) is similar in appearance to both the Buff-necked Ibis and the Black-faced Ibis but is the only one of the three found in high-altitude habitats in the tropical Andes. Some authorities considered it conspecific with the Black-faced Ibis until relatively recently. It is uncommon in high-altitude páramo and is unmistakable in its range. Antisana Ecological Reserve in Ecuador is a good place to find it.

CONSERVATION — THE PÁRAMO

One Endemic Bird Area is dedicated to the páramo, the Central Andean Páramo, which includes parts of the highlands of Colombia and Ecuador. Fortunately, relatively few globally threatened bird species specialize in páramo habitats. Two examples, though, are the striking Buffy and Blue-bearded Helmetcrests of Colombia (which are Vulnerable and Endangered, respectively). Some other species, such as the Vulnerable Rufous-fronted Parakeet and the Black-breasted Puffleg and Dusky Starfrontlet, both Endangered, are found close to or on the edge of páramo in elfin and cloud forests.

It appears that the current extent of páramo grasslands is somewhat defined by historical anthropogenic factors, such as the grazing of llamas, since the boundary between forest and grassland often seems artificially linear. Nevertheless, while grazing still takes place in these areas, páramo tends to be less threatened than other Andean life zones. This is likely because the ecosystem is generally high, wet, and cold and is not especially good for farming or livestock grazing. A number of large, fairly well-protected reserves also cover significant amounts of páramo habitat. These include the Antisana Ecological Reserve in Ecuador, and Los Nevados National Park and the Sierra Nevada de Santa Marta National Natural Park in Colombia, which also protect important páramo habitat—including for the recently rediscovered and Critically Endangered Blue-bearded Helmetcrest. The latter park overlaps a number of indigenous territories and is primarily operated by these communities. In Ecuador, another Critically Endangered páramo hummingbird, the recently discovered Blue-throated Hillstar, is now protected by a new Fundación Jocotoco reserve at Cerro de Arcos, supported by American Bird Conservancy.

ECUADORIAN HILLSTAR (*Oreotrochilus chimborazo*) is almost endemic to Ecuador (it is recorded from just a few locations in southern Colombia) and is found at elevations up to 15,000 feet (female pictured). These beautiful hummingbirds are strongly associated with the orange-colored flowers of *Chuquiragua* shrubs and can often be seen feeding on them. The birds vary from highly mobile to almost inactive while feeding—when they often perch on or close to the flowers—so they can be hard to find and pin down for a picture. The violet gleam of the male's throat in the right light is absolutely stunning.

BIRDING AND PHOTOGRAPHY SITES — THE PÁRAMO

In Ecuador, Antisana Ecological Reserve is one of the best places to experience páramo habitat. The reserve is based around the Antisana volcano and covers a range of habitats, including high peaks, lakes, *Polylepis* forest, and significant areas of tussock grasslands. It is a great place to see such birds as Andean Ibis, Carunculated Caracara, Andean Tit-Spinetail, Silvery Grebe, Andean Gull, and Ecuadorian Hillstar (in the low shrubs around the reserve center, for example). If you kneel down to photograph birds, be sure to protect your knees from stinging plants.

No visit to Antisana would be complete without a side trip to Fundación Jocotoco's nearby reserve at Chakana. The cliffs here (which can be watched from an observation deck along the road) have roosting Andean Condors that are best seen early in the morning before they begin to drift away to search for food. Just before you reach the observation deck (driving from Quito), a small restaurant called Tambo Condor on the left has feeders that attract Giant Hummingbirds, among other species. The reserve at Chakana is also a good place to see Ecuadorian Hillstars visiting the *Chuquiraga* flowers along the road before the hairpin turn, as well as, occasionally, spectacled bears—which can be found foraging on the slopes below the cliff or on the road up to the reserve center, feeding on the abundant bromeliads that cloak the hillsides. Another well-known páramo site is Papallacta Pass, also in Ecuador. The pass is easily reached from Quito and has a good representation of typical páramo birds, such as Tawny Antpitta and Rufous-bellied Seedsnipe. Farther south in Ecuador, at Cerro de Arcos, birders have the chance to see typical páramo species alongside the recently discovered spectacular Blue-throated Hillstar. One of the best places to see and photograph Andean Condors in the tropical Andes is at Colca Canyon, northwest of Arequipa, Peru. The birds often soar close to an observation area there and may also perch atop the cliffs close to the road.

CARUNCULATED CARACARA (*Phalcoboenus carunculatus*) is found at altitudes from 10,000 to 13,000 feet in the Andes of southern Colombia and Ecuador. It is replaced by the similar Mountain Caracara to the south from Peru to Chile. The Carunculated has darker, more streaked underparts, however. These caracaras can be seen on the open páramo at sites such as the Antisana Ecological Reserve, in Ecuador. They often hop around, foraging in between the cushion plants and tussock grasses, and appear to fill the ecological niche occupied by corvids, such as ravens, in North America. These caracaras can sometimes be seen alongside condors scavenging on animal carcasses.

YELLOW-BILLED PINTAIL (*Anas georgica*) is an elegant duck that is strongly reminiscent of a female Northern Pintail—though note that in this species, the sexes are similar, unlike the male and female Northern Pintail. These stately waterfowl are commonly found on high-altitude lakes and may occur together with Yellow-billed Teal (which have a darker head and are more compact overall). This beautiful pintail is more widespread in the southern part of South America and can be found at a greater variety of altitudes there than in the northern part of its range.

STOUT-BILLED CINCLODES (*Cinclodes excelsior*) is a high-altitude species that is found in grasslands and páramo at elevations up to 15,000 feet or more in the highlands of Colombia and Ecuador. These birds are usually conspicuous and noisy as they forage around rocks, shrubs, and *Polylepis* trees at locations such as Jocotoco's Chakana Reserve, in the Ecuadorian Andes not far from Quito. They nest in burrows in earthen banks, including alongside pastures.

MASKED FLOWERPIERCER (*Diglossa cyanea*) is a common and widespread species found in forest at altitudes up to about 12,000 feet on both slopes of the Andes, and it ranges from Colombia to Bolivia. Its behavior is similar to that of other flowerpiercers, but Masked is thought to be more frugivorous than some of the smaller species. Its beady red eye provides a striking focal point for photographs, and Zuroloma, in Ecuador, is among the best places to see and photograph this species.

POLYLEPIS FOREST › BIOGEOGRAPHY AND HISTORY

More than forty species of *Polylepis* trees range across the Andes from Venezuela to Chile and Argentina. Though you would not know it by looking at them, *Polylepis* trees are part of the rose family. *Polylepis* forest tends to occur in small, isolated patches, rather than in extensive woodlands. It is frequently found in sheltered coves or enclosed valleys or canyons, but almost always at very high altitudes. In some areas, the trees can grow quite large, but the typical *Polylepis* tree tends to have the look of a wizened bonsai, with multiple gnarled branches, and it often has a windswept aspect that conjures the image of a forest from a science-fantasy novel. The trees are characterized by many layers of paper-thin bark that flakes off easily and a reddish-colored trunk with tiny, dark green leaves. The science-fantasy aspect is often amplified by the frequent understory of lush green moss, often surrounded by tussock grass on the higher edges of the páramo or elfin forest. While *Polylepis* is widespread across the Andes, the Cordillera Blanca and Apurimac-Cusco regions of Peru, and the Cochabamba area in Bolivia are especially important from a bird conservation point of view, since several rare or endangered endemics that are tied to *Polylepis* forest are found in these areas.

Polylepis doesn't necessarily equate to a region that can be described from a cultural perspective, but the epicenter of bird endemism in *Polylepis* equates almost precisely to the area of greatest influence of the Incan Empire. In fact, most communities that live in the vicinity of these forests tend to speak Quechua or Aymara as a first language and often dress in the colorful garb typical of high-altitude communities descended from the Incas. In fact, one of the *Polylepis* forest areas best known to birders is quite close to Machu Picchu itself. It lies on the far side of the mountain known in Quechua as Huacayhuilki (later renamed "Veronica" by Spanish colonists), which is visible from the sundial at the top of the citadel—only eleven miles as the cincloides flies from the citadel itself. There are multiple theories as to what happened to the residents of Machu Picchu. One that has not been widely discussed is that the population may have just abandoned it after the Spanish invasion and blended into the surrounding hills—in such a case, their descendants would therefore be the current residents of such villages as Thastayoc, which lies right above the classic *Polylepis* birding site at Abra Malaga. Whatever the true fate of the citadel's people, it is undoubtedly true that the Incas were intimately familiar with these areas and with *Polylepis* forest, and that modern Quechua culture still bears many of the hallmarks of traditional Inca life. These mountains are also the original home of the potato, and multiple varieties are still cooked together by burying them with burning embers to properly roast them. Local communities still grow giant-kernel corn, drink *chicha*, an alcoholic beverage made from fermented corn, and eat *cuy*—cooked guinea pig—which is considered a delicacy in the region.

BROWN-BACKED CHAT-TYRANT (*Ochthoeca fumicolor*) is a widespread species that occurs from Venezuela to Bolivia and is found above 9,000 feet in open areas and shrubby páramo. Like most chat-tyrants, these birds tend to perch atop prominent bushes or sticks, from which they hunt insects—sallying either into the air or to the ground. They tend to flick their tails in alarm but can also be confiding if approached carefully.

POLYLEPIS FOREST: BIRD DIVERSITY AND SPECIALTIES

Polylepis forest harbors some of the most interesting and rarest birds in the Andes. Perhaps the most sought after and celebrated of these is the Critically Endangered Royal Cinclodes of southeastern Peru and northwestern Bolivia. In recent years, the species has been found farther north into central Peru, in the Junín region, but it is still incredibly rare and hard to see. Given that it lives at about 14,000 feet in altitude, it is also a challenge for most people who live at sea level to hike at these elevations without acclimatization. The cinclodes is just one of a range of globally threatened birds that are found in these forests. Two other threatened *Polylepis* obligates are the White-browed Tit-Spinetail and the Ash-breasted Tit-Tyrant. All three of these species often occur together and are typical of *Polylepis* habitat. A more widespread species that is also almost completely tied to *Polylepis* is the Giant Conebill. This nuthatch-like bark forager can sometimes be heard before it is seen as it shimmies up and down the flaky trunks in groups hunting for insects. Another typical species of this habitat is the Stripe-headed Antpitta—one of the smaller members of the *Grallaria* antpitta group and also one of the easier of these species to see in the field.

These forests also have a strong supporting cast of high-altitude birds, species such as the tiny Vilcabamba Tapaculo, the Olivaceous Thornbill, Scarlet-bellied Mountain Tanager, Thick-billed and Black Siskins, Mountain Caracara, Andean Condor, and a range of ground-tyrants and sierra finches. Close to Cochabamba, Bolivia, in Tunari National Park, it is also possible to find the large and spectacularly colored Cochabamba Mountain Finch. This species has an even more restricted distribution than the Royal Cinclodes, although it is relatively easier to see, as it occurs close to roads and skulks somewhat less. The Puente San Miguel area on the road from Cochabamba to Tunari is an especially good place to find it. Visitors to this area may also be rewarded with sightings of the spectacular Red-tailed Comet, Great Pampa-Finch, Red-crested Cotinga, Olive-crowned Crescentchest, and Rufous-bellied Mountain Tanager in the trees and shrubs that cloak the steep slopes on either side of the road.

RUFOUS-SIDED WARBLING FINCH (*Poospizopsis hypochondria*) is actually more closely related to tanagers than to finches and is found primarily from central Bolivia to northern Argentina in high-altitude scrubby habitats, often associated with *Polylepis* forest. It occurs at altitudes from about 7,000 feet to nearly 13,000 feet.

CONSERVATION — POLYLEPIS FOREST

Polylepis woodland is spread out across the Andes from Venezuela to Tierra del Fuego and included in multiple Endemic Bird Areas and Important Bird Areas. The Peruvian High Andes and the High Andes of Bolivia and Argentina are two Endemic Bird Areas of particular importance to the habitat. Globally threatened species using *Polylepis* include the Critically Endangered Royal Cinclodes and the White-browed Tit-Spinetail and Ash-breasted Tit-Tyrant, both of which are Endangered. Other *Polylepis* species, such as the White-cheeked Cotinga and Cochabamba Mountain Finch (both Near-Threatened), are also of potential conservation concern.

The conservation of *Polylepis* woodland was at the bottom of most conservation organizations' to-do lists until about 2000, when a partnership between American Bird Conservancy and ECOAN (Asociación Ecosistemas Andinos), the Peruvian conservation group, started to focus on these habitats. With early support from the Alton Jones Foundation, ECOAN and American Bird Conservancy embarked on a project in the Vilcanota Mountains of southeastern Peru to conserve a critical site for *Polylepis* birds known as Abra Malaga. Since then, the project has grown to include a number of surrounding communities and has supported the creation of multiple protected areas run by indigenous people. The project has also focused on reforesting the reserves with *Polylepis* saplings and has now planted more than ten million trees in total across the Andes.

More recently, the project has evolved into an initiative known as Acción Andina with the support of Global Forest Generation, which seeks to reforest 2.5 million acres of the Andes with *Polylepis* trees through a multicountry collaboration. The original focal species—Royal Cinclodes, Ash-breasted Tit-Tyrant, and White-browed Tit-Spinetail—are still present at the project's first focal site more than twenty years after the extinction of at least the cinclodes first seemed imminent. The project was recently awarded a prestigious Earthshot Prize by Prince William to expand its scope, and it has been named a United Nations World Restoration flagship.

GIANT CONEBILL (*Conirostrum binghami*) is one of the most charismatic birds of the *Polylepis* forest. Widely distributed from Ecuador to Bolivia (with reports from northern Chile and Argentina), this unique species is often on the must-see list for keen birders, as it is such a characteristic *Polylepis* obligate. These birds superficially look like nuthatches, and they behave like them, too—gleaning insects from the flaky layers of *Polylepis* bark. You can sometimes hear them before you see them, as they rustle the bark of the trees while feeding in small groups.

BIRDING AND PHOTOGRAPHY SITES | POLYLEPIS FOREST

The classic location for birding in *Polylepis* forest is still the site known as Abra Malaga. It lies in southeastern Peru within a few hours' drive of Cusco. The site was historically known as *the* place to see Royal Cinclodes. It is now a local community-operated reserve, and visitors must pay a small fee to enter. These fees are used to support conservation actions and to help provide resources for community members. The site lies at about 14,000 feet in altitude, so it is essential to acclimatize if you are early in a trip and are used to living at sea level. The hike to look for the birds starts with a gentle-enough rise but then crests a hill from which a *Polylepis* forest is visible in the valley far below the ridge. A trail goes down to the forest, and you can also leave the site by continuing down the valley to the southeast, rather than climbing back up the hill (the valley is a much longer walk, however). Visitors may see the cinclodes, tit-tyrant, and tit-spinetail anywhere on the descent through the tussock grass-covered slopes, which have many small clusters of *Polylepis* trees, but it can also require a trip to the very bottom of the valley, and even then, the cinclodes is not guaranteed. The return walk from the bottom of the valley to the ridge can be grueling for those who have not acclimatized.

If you bird this area, make sure to include a visit to the cloud forest on the opposite side of the Abra Malaga pass from Ollantaytambo. This area, known historically to birders as Carrizales, has nice scrubby forest and bamboo, where you can find birds such as Plushcap, Sword-billed Hummingbird, Red-crested Cotinga, Tit-like Dacnis, Inca Wren, and Red-and-white and Urubamba Antpittas. Keep a lookout for the large trumpet flowers (*Datura* or *Brugmansia*) that Sword-billed Hummingbirds feed on. Another key site for *Polylepis* birds is the lower reaches of Tunari National Park near Cochabamba, Bolivia. The key species here is Cochabamba Mountain Finch, which can best be found in the complex of small fields and stone walls around Puente San Miguel, located immediately before the road from Cochabamba to Tunari crosses the river and climbs through several sharp switchbacks (look down to the river from the bridge to catch a glimpse, with luck, of a White-capped Dipper!).

While many other *Polylepis* areas are good for birding, including areas in northern Bolivia where Royal Cinclodes can also be found, the last one I will mention here is Papallacta Pass in Ecuador. Lying east of Quito along Highway E28, the *Polylepis* forest around the pass can be a good place to find Giant Conebills, and while this species also occurs at Abra Malaga, I have not seen it there despite multiple visits. It is also present in Tunari but is reportedly also becoming rarer in that area. In Peru, I have found the species only in valleys neighboring Abra Malaga, such as Yanahuara, but this requires a much more significant hike and potentially overnight camping, whereas at Papallacta, the forest is much more readily accessible and much closer to the road. Other birds found at Papallacta include the Masked Mountain Tanager, Black-backed Bush Tanager, and Shining Sunbeam.

COCHABAMBA MOUNTAIN FINCH (*Poospiza garleppi*) is a large, distinctive species with a narrow global range that is strongly associated with *Polylepis* forest at altitudes above about 10,000 feet. Scientific analysis has shown that this species is a tanager, not a finch. An excellent place to see it is along the road to Tunari National Park from Cochabamba, Bolivia, where this photo was taken. BirdLife International considers it Near Threatened. COUNTRY ENDEMIC (BOLIVIA)

FULVOUS-HEADED BRUSHFINCH

(*Atlapetes fulviceps*) is one of the most distinctive members of its genus and occurs in higher-altitude montane forests and associated scrub, including in *Polylepis* woodland, from central Bolivia to Argentina. These birds are sometimes encountered within mixed flocks and tend to forage in the understory. The species replaces the Bolivian Brushfinch south of the humid yungas on the East Slope of the Bolivian Andes.

TYRIAN METALTAIL

(*Metallura tyrianthina*) is a small, active, short-billed hummingbird. The males lack strong distinguishing marks aside from their distinctive coppery-red tail. Females, though, have a buffy throat and chest, which tend to make them more immediately recognizable. This metaltail is found in scrubby areas and along forest edge above 7,500 feet and is relatively common, frequently visiting feeders, including those at Zuroloma, in Ecuador. The species can be found from Venezuela to Bolivia.

> **FROM THE FIELD** — *Personal stories from the leaders of American Bird Conservancy's primary bird and habitat conservation partners in the tropical Andes.*

A CHAMPION FOR CONSERVATION IN PERU LAUNCHES AN ANDES-WIDE CONSERVATION CAMPAIGN

FOR HIGH ANDEAN communities, birds are descendants of the great Inca culture, mythological beings, revered and highly appreciated, because birds connect the earthly world with the heavenly world inhabited by the gods. In 1989, Dr. Jon Fjeldså and I explored the Peruvian Andes of Ayacucho and Apurimac Departments during Jon's work to complete the book *Birds of the High Andes*. Mindful of guerrillas, mountains, *Polylepis* forests, and local communities in these areas, I took on the commitment, with encouragement from Jon, to work on the conservation of these native forests and the region's biodiversity and to work with local communities (which had been asking for respect and to be a part of the solution to the region's environmental problems). Reviving ancestral practices to achieve conservation outcomes was central to my mission. It was a big responsibility and became the foundation of the nongovernmental organization ECOAN (Asociación Ecosistemas Andinos) and, later, Acción Andina.

Between 1990 and 1999, I worked with my colleagues to research *Polylepis* forests and all the fauna and flora that inhabit them in the Vilcanota, Apurimac, and Vilcabamba Mountains, enjoying friendship and Andean culture along the journey. In the year 2000, my colleagues from Cusco (Gregorio Ferro, Efrain Samochuallpa, and Wily Palomino) and I founded ECOAN with the mission of conserving Andean ecosystems and their threatened species, and with the specific goal of doing so in coordination with local people and for the benefit of local and native communities.

The beginning years of ECOAN were very hard, since no one believed in this mission. Everyone was busy protecting conservation corridors and hotspots and creating protected areas, but, unfortunately, deforestation was still winning the battle. Only American Bird Conservancy supported ECOAN from the beginning. In 2000, Mike Parr arrived in Cusco to speak with me and work together conserving the threatened species and birds of Peru. We worked hard and grew together as a family, and after twenty-three years, we can congratulate ourselves on everything we have achieved. American Bird Conservancy, with George and Rita Fenwick at the helm, chose to support ECOAN, and real, concrete, and on-the-ground actions have increased and secured the habitat of numerous species, stabilizing and increasing their populations. Local communities work on species conservation because they feel respected and happy to be part of the solution to the problem.

In the last decade, many institutions have included the social component in their missions, since it was impossible to ignore it. New generations of conservationists are trained by ECOAN. It all started by conserving species and was possible with the support of many allies and donors. After decades of work, the communities are engaged and especially focused on conserving habitat to provide clean water. The women say, "Water is life, economy, and the future of our children." By ensuring water and its biodiversity, we conserve ecosystems and generate more hope for species, people, and the planet. Highly threatened species need many years of adaptation to respond to new changes in their habitat. Conservation is not a job that lasts a couple of years but is a cyclical issue that requires medium- to long-term programs.

ECOAN and American Bird Conservancy are protecting a large number of threatened and iconic species in Peru, and building local capacity, providing jobs, and empowering many local people underpin their success at the national and international level. Both institutions have understood that it is only following through on commitments that guarantees the success of conservation.

CONSTANTINO AUCCA CHUTAS
President, ECOAN

SWORD-BILLED HUMMINGBIRD (*Ensifera ensifera*) is one of the most sought-after and distinctive of all Andean birds. This species can regularly be seen attending the hummingbird feeders at ECOAN's Abra Patricia reserve in northern Peru close to the Alto Mayo Protection Forest. The lodge is also a great place to see some of the rarest restricted-range species of the region, including the Long-whiskered Owlet, Royal Sunangel, and Bar-winged Wood-Wren.

THE ALTIPLANO AND PUNA

BLACK-HOODED SIERRA FINCH (*Phrygilus atriceps*) replaces the Peruvian Sierra Finch in southern Peru, Bolivia, and Chile. The male of this stunning high-altitude species has a blacker head and warmer mantle and underparts than the Peruvian. Black-hooded Sierra Finches (female pictured) can be found in open areas with small bushes, as well as around habitation. They are usually found in pairs or small flocks and are regularly seen foraging on the ground or in low shrubs and other vegetation.

THE ALTIPLANO AND PUNA > BIOGEOGRAPHY AND HISTORY

The altiplano—literally the "high plains" in Spanish—is a large area of the high Andes that extends from Peru into Bolivia and, farther south, slightly into both Chile and Argentina. While most experts agree that the altiplano really begins in southeastern Peru in the vicinity of Lake Titicaca, there are significant elements of puna in central Peru around Lake Junín, and even farther north. The altiplano is much more extensive in Bolivia than elsewhere, as the structure of the Andes there creates a vast, open, high-altitude plain in between a multitude of volcanoes, unlike the generally single cordillera that crosses Ecuador and Peru. The puna is more vegetated than the true altiplano, but there can be a gradation between altiplano and puna, and between puna-like habitats and páramo—which tends to be more humid and have more tussock grass and small shrubs than true puna (and it lies farther north—see the páramo section). Several types of puna have been described, including Humid and Desert Grassland Puna and Succulent Puna. The altiplano is characterized by its altitude—typically above 12,000 feet—by its desert-like aspect, and, in many places, by significant volcanic activity. There are numerous high-altitude lakes associated with the altiplano, the largest and deepest of which is Lake Titicaca, which is about one hundred miles in extent along its longest axis. Lake Junín in central Peru is also of significant size; with its surrounding marshes, it is about thirty miles long. The large, shallow Lake Poopó, which lies about 175 miles southeast of Lake Titicaca, almost completely dried up in 2015 due to water diversion and climate change and may never recover. Many of the remaining high-altitude lakes are also extremely shallow and are found close to (and mainly south of) the extensive salt pans of southwestern Bolivia. These salt pans, formed by the drying of prehistoric lakes, contain some of the world's largest lithium deposits, and are consequently under threat from development, since lithium is widely used in the production of batteries for electric cars and in the development of renewable energy.

While the true altiplano is most frequently almost devoid of vegetation, the puna (which tends to become drier as you move south) is characterized by bunch grasses such as *Stipa*, *Festuca*, and *Calamagrostis*; cushion plants such as *Azorella* and *Distichia*; and feathergrasses. Another characteristic plant of these altitudes is the giant Queen of the Andes (*Puya raimondii*), a bromeliad used by hummingbirds and canasteros with an inflorescence that grows to twenty feet or more in height. People who live at or close to sea level commonly find the altitudes at which these habitats are found challenging to adapt to quickly, and it is often better to ascend gradually by choosing a mid-elevation destination where you can stage and acclimatize, rather than traveling directly to Puno, Peru, or Uyuni, Bolivia, for example.

The puna is also strongly associated with the distribution of the vicuña, the world's smallest camelid, and the Lesser or Puna Rhea. Both species likely are leading prey species for pumas, which are also found, though rarely seen, in these habitats. Both the altiplano and puna are xeric systems that receive little seasonal rain and can become desert-like, with just patches of isolated shrubs on otherwise bare earth, in parts of southern Bolivia. Such areas are fairly devoid of birds except for the occasional Puna Tinamou or Ash-breasted Sierra Finch. Due to the altitude and cold, precipitation may fall as snow, and this is most likely to be encountered in the wet season from about December to March. Visitors may encounter small bogs called *bofedales*, which tend to attract good numbers of such birds as Andean Geese, cinclodes, sierra finches, and others.

The region's cultural history is similar to that of the southeastern dry foothills, in that it has seen control pass from the early Tiahuanaco Empire centered around Lake Titicaca to the Aymara, then to the Incas, and finally to the Spanish before the modern nations were founded. One cultural group, the Uru or Uros, now live mostly on floating reed islands in Lake Titicaca. Their communities depend almost entirely on totora reeds for home and boat construction. They also depend on fishing and on modest income from tourists who visit the Uros islands by boat from Puno, Peru. Among other things, this income has helped to pay for solar panels that reduce fire risk on the reed islands and help to power televisions and other conveniences. At first glance, the colorful clothing of the Uros has much in common with that worn by Quechua-speaking communities, but many of the Uros also speak the ancient Aymara language. Clothing in these regions is highly symbolic, and the style and color of garments can hold important meaning, such as whether the wearer is single or married, for example.

PUNA TEAL (*Spatula puna*) is a familiar bird of the highland lakes and wetlands. Its striking dark cap and blue bill are both distinctive and elegant. It is frequently found in the company of other high-altitude-lake ducks, such as the Yellow-billed Pintail and Crested Duck. It is one of several species of Andean duck in which the sexes are similar.

BIRD DIVERSITY AND SPECIALTIES › THE ALTIPLANO AND PUNA

The birds of the altiplano and puna ecosystems are a hardy bunch, squeezing a living out of a dry and sparsely vegetated high-altitude plain. Despite this, the region has significant avian diversity and really unique and fascinating species. Among the most characteristic birds are several species of earthcreepers, miners, cinclodes, canasteros, shrike-tyrants, ground-tyrants, and sierra finches. The region's high Andean lakes and marshes also have a range of distinctive species, including the colorful Many-colored Rush Tyrant, the Wren-like Rushbird, and the Plumbeous Rail (which are all also found along the Peruvian coast). Both Lake Junín and Lake Titicaca have endemic grebe species. The Titicaca Grebe is distinctive, and there are no confusion species on the lake. On the other hand, care must be taken in identifying the Junin Grebe because the similar-looking Silvery Grebe is also common on Lake Junín. It is usually impossible to separate them reliably from the lake's shore, since the open water is some distance from any reasonable vantage point due to the lake's fringing marshes. Instead, arrange for a boat trip out of Ondores that will get you close to the birds and allow them to be readily identified (the Junin Grebe is larger and longer-billed and has whiter flanks). Lake Junín also has a unique form of Black Rail that some authorities split. Surprisingly, this can be reliably seen with help from a local bird guide, who can also assist with the boat tour. To explore the area, contact Cesar Donato Zevallos Bashualdo via Facebook.

High Andean lakes also provide important stopover and wintering habitat for migratory shorebirds such as the Baird's Sandpiper, Pectoral Sandpiper, Wilson's Phalarope, American Golden-Plover, and Lesser Yellowlegs. The spectacular Andean Avocet can also be found on these lakes and along some of the region's few watercourses, although rarely in large numbers. Two other unique shorebirds found in the region are the Tawny-throated Dotterel and the Diademed Sandpiper-Plover. The dotterel can be found in open fields—for example, in the Titicaca region—and the sandpiper-plover near high-altitude bogs adjacent to puna and rocky areas. Several other species are associated with these high-elevation lakes and bogs, including Chilean, Andean, and James's Flamingos, Andean Negrito, Andean Gull, Puna Snipe, Puna Teal, Yellow-billed Pintail, Crested Duck, Puna Ibis, Puna Plover, Andean Lapwing, and Giant Coot.

Other birds that can be encountered while birding these highlands include Correndera Pipit, Black Siskin, Andean Flicker, Mountain Caracara, Aplomado Falcon, Giant Hummingbird, Andean Hillstar, Red-tailed Comet, Glacier Finch (which has been found nesting in crevices in glaciers), Golden-spotted and Black-winged Ground Doves, Rufous-bellied and Gray-breasted Seedsnipes, Puna and Taczanowski's Tinamous, Puna Yellow-Finch, and Andean Ibis.

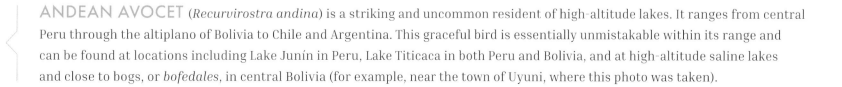

ANDEAN AVOCET (*Recurvirostra andina*) is a striking and uncommon resident of high-altitude lakes. It ranges from central Peru through the altiplano of Bolivia to Chile and Argentina. This graceful bird is essentially unmistakable within its range and can be found at locations including Lake Junín in Peru, Lake Titicaca in both Peru and Bolivia, and at high-altitude saline lakes and close to bogs, or *bofedales*, in central Bolivia (for example, near the town of Uyuni, where this photo was taken).

THE ALTIPLANO AND PUNA > CONSERVATION

Two Endemic Bird Areas are focused strongly on the puna: the Junín Puna in Peru and the High Andes of Bolivia and Argentina. In Peru, both the Junin Grebe and Rail are considered to be globally Endangered, as is the Titicaca Grebe. The most endangered bird of the highest elevations is the Critically Endangered White-bellied Cinclodes, which now appears to be confined to a small area of peat bog in the vicinity of Ticlio, Peru, and to similar habitats in the vicinity. Other species, such as Taczanowski's Tinamou and Andean Flamingo, are considered to be globally Vulnerable, but given the impacts of climate change and the potential for mining impacts, perhaps James's Flamingo should be considered for an upgrade from Near-Threatened as well.

In Peru, both Lake Junín and Lake Titicaca are protected, but the same is not yet true for the Bolivian side of Titicaca, and while Lake Poopó is protected, upstream and climate effects cannot be contained by protected areas alone, and the lake has all but dried up. There are a number of additional protected areas in the altiplano, including the important Eduardo Avaroa Andean Fauna National Reserve in Bolivia, which protects key flamingo nesting areas in the altiplano, as well as Lauca National Park in northern Chile. ECOAN (Asociación Ecosistemas Andinos) is also working with American Bird Conservancy's support to implement additional conservation measures for Lake Junín and to save the grebe and rail from extinction.

The high Andes have been densely settled for centuries, although until modern times, human impacts have been limited mostly to the domestication of llamas (descended from wild guanacos) and alpacas for grazing, and a relatively limited amount of agriculture and settlement. Much of the altiplano does not provide ideal land for grazing or farming, and it has mostly been spared from habitat change at the hands of people until recently. In recent years, mining has begun to have a significant impact on bird habitat in parts of central Peru, and peat removal is also damaging high-altitude bogs in the region. The northwestern end of Lake Junín has been seriously harmed by mine runoff and is heavily polluted, although this appears to affect only a relatively small part of the lake so far, fortunately. Lake Titicaca is also quite polluted around Puno, and the Titicaca Grebe is less common in that area—although it is still fairly widespread on the lake as a whole (and on surrounding lakes). The introduction of trout to some high Andean lakes has hampered conservation efforts, and climate change is beginning to affect the high Andes as well. For example, Lake Poopó in Bolivia has mostly dried up as a result of this and of water diversion. Aside from this continuing desiccation from global warming, a potential threat to the high-altitude salt pans of Bolivia is the mining of lithium. Bolivia has some of the largest lithium deposits in the world, and these primarily lie beneath salt flats on the altiplano. It is ironic that these areas are threatened both by climate change itself and by human efforts to reduce climate change from mined lithium, which is used in electric car batteries and in renewable energy development. While renewables are essential in the fight against climate change, the impacts of renewable development must be considered as well as their benefits. Nevertheless, overall, Bolivia has one of the most extensive networks of protected areas in the region, with 167 protected areas covering nearly 31 percent of its national territory. Moreover, the salt pans themselves are relatively devoid of birdlife (though they are used by flamingos in the wet season), and mining has had limited impact so far.

JAMES'S FLAMINGO (*Phoenicoparrus jamesi*) is a rare resident of very high-altitude lakes. It ranges from central Bolivia to Chile and Argentina (and is a nonbreeding visitor to Peru); large concentrations of individuals are found at both Laguna Hedionda and Laguna Colorada, in southern Bolivia. These attractive birds often gather with large numbers of Andean and Chilean Flamingos on breeding lakes in some of the harshest and least hospitable areas of the planet.

BIRDING AND PHOTOGRAPHY SITES — THE ALTIPLANO AND PUNA

The altiplano is replete with great birding and bird photography locations. The drive from Lima to Lake Junín passes through many wonderful birding areas. The old Santa Eulalia Road traverses a number of ecotones, finally reaching an area of peat bog (*bofedales*) around Marcapomacocha that is a classic location for Diademed Sandpiper-Plover. These birds are not always found here reliably, but there are lots of other great birds to find in the area, including earthcreepers, Rufous-bellied Seedsnipe, Puna Tinamou, and, potentially, White-bellied Cinclodes. Lake Junín is a site of outstanding natural beauty and incredible wildlife. The entire area is quite birdy, with lots of sierra finches, ground doves, shrike-tyrants, Andean Flickers, Mountain Caracaras, and other typical high-altitude birds. It is critical to rent a boat at Ondores to get out on the lake to see Junin Grebe properly; the trip might also include views of Andean Avocet, Andean Goose, Chilean Flamingo, Andean Duck, Slate-colored Coot; or thousands of Wilson's Phalaropes, depending on the season. On the way back to Lima, stop at the high pass at Ticlio for another chance to find White-bellied Cinclodes, Rufous-bellied Seedsnipe, and Diademed Sandpiper-Plover. Meanwhile, check the small lake below the pass for Giant Coot.

At Lake Titicaca, the marshes at the northwestern end of the lake tend to be better for birding, but, again, a boat rental is virtually essential to get close to waterbirds such as the endemic grebe and, potentially, Andean Avocets and other high-altitude lake species. The fields around the lake sometimes hold Tawny-throated Dotterel, but to see any, it may be necessary to drive around while scanning.

Farther south, areas around Uyuni and a drive out across the salt pans to the puna and more remote locations, such as Laguna Hedionda or Laguna Colorada, can yield views of Lesser or Puna Rhea, and the lakes themselves and some surrounding lakes are excellent for all three species of Andean flamingo: Chilean, Andean, and James's. The rheas can often be seen most easily in cultivated fields to the south of Uyuni, rather than in the vast expanse of the natural altiplano. These areas are very far above sea level, and for most people it is critical to acclimatize at mid-elevations prior to birding actively in the puna and altiplano. Locations such as Cusco, Peru, and Cochabamba, Bolivia, can be ideal for this. It is not advisable to take the Central Highway to Ticlio and Junín immediately after arriving in Lima, since the trip requires cresting a pass at more than 16,000 feet in elevation. Instead, build up to it by starting in Cusco or Machu Picchu; then head higher once you have acclimatized. The altiplano can also be very cold, although it is important to prepare for bright sun as well as the potential for snow. Despite the physical challenges of the environment, the high altiplano and puna boast some of the most iconic and unusual birds of the high Andes and are well worth the effort.

> **LESSER RHEA** (*Rhea pennata*) is the second largest bird in South America by weight and height. (It is surpassed only by its lowland counterpart, the Greater Rhea.) The Lesser Rhea is found from Peru to Chile in the high altiplano at altitudes above 12,000 feet, and usually higher. Its favored habitat is extremely arid and desert-like, with little vegetation except for a few small shrubs. It is most frequently found in small groups and can be seen in agricultural fields as well as in the open puna.

GREAT THRUSH (*Turdus fuscater*) is a large, dark, conspicuous thrush found from Colombia to Bolivia. While the smaller and browner Chiguanco Thrush overlaps in range, the Great Thrush tends to prefer more humid forest-edge environments, rather than more arid and open areas. Nevertheless, "Is that a Great Thrush or a Chiguanco Thrush?" is a question often asked by birders on trips to the Andes.

PLUMBEOUS SIERRA FINCH (*Geospizopsis unicolor*) is a widespread species and familiar to birders who visit the high Andes. Except for the pink legs and black eyes, males are almost completely gray, but they can sometimes have a bluish look to them in flight. Females (pictured) are brown and streaky, reminiscent of a rosefinch, House Finch, or siskin (although they tend to be grayer in the southern part of their range). Found from Venezuela to Argentina, this species usually occurs at altitudes above 10,000 feet, but its southernmost populations can be found closer to sea level.

PUNA IBIS (*Plegadis ridgwayi*) is a typical, though stocky, *Plegadis* ibis, like the Glossy and White-faced that are familiar to North American birders. This species occupies the gap between those two species in South America, where Glossies are found in the north and White-faced in the south. The Puna Ibis can be found from the highlands of Ecuador to northern Argentina and has an interesting distribution, in that it occupies both high puna and coastal areas.

ANDEAN GOOSE (*Oressochen melanopterus*) is another distinctive species that is typically found in pairs or small groups in *bofedales* (Andean bogs) at altitudes above 12,000 feet from Peru to Chile. While sexes are similar in plumage, males are much larger than females.

GRAY-BREASTED SEEDSNIPE (*Thinocorus orbignyianus*) is one of the world's four species of seedsnipe, all of which are confined to South America. These unusual birds are reminiscent of game birds such as quail or ptarmigan but are more closely related to shorebirds. This species is similar in appearance to the Least Seedsnipe of the coast but is confined to high-altitude environments. Gray-breasted is more frequently encountered than its relative, the Rufous-bellied Seedsnipe, and seems to be more adaptable to a range of habitats.

CREAM-WINGED CINCLODES
(*Cinclodes albiventris*) is one of three species that were formerly grouped as the Bar-winged Cinclodes. Cream-winged is found in the southern tropical Andes, with Chestnut-winged to its north in Ecuador and Colombia and Buff-winged to its south—primarily in central and southern Chile and Argentina. This individual was photographed in Bolivia's Tunari National Park, outside the city of Cochabamba.

HOODED SISKIN
(*Spinus magellanicus*) is the common siskin across most of the Andes from Colombia to Chile and occurs in a range of open habitats, including agricultural areas, fields, and small, forested groves. These small, colorful finches are often seen in flocks and most often are first detected by their distinctive, wheezy, squeaky calls. Several other siskin species in the region are similar in appearance, including the Saffron, Olivaceous, and Thick-billed, and these often require care to separate in the field.

ANDEAN LAPWING (*Vanellus resplendens*) replaces the Southern Lapwing at higher altitudes and can be recognized easily, as it lacks the crest and broad black chest band of its lower-elevation counterpart. The Andean Lapwing is fairly common in open areas, in agricultural fields and pastures, and in marshy areas in the uplands. It occurs from Colombia to Chile and forms small flocks outside the breeding season, only very occasionally ranging to the coast or into Amazonia.

YELLOW-BILLED TEAL (*Anas flavirostris*) is another subtly beautiful duck that is found on the region's high-altitude lakes. These birds are more widely distributed in the southern part of their range outside the Andes. The Andean birds differ from other populations of the species in having paler gray flanks. When seen well, the delicate vermiculation and spots of this species are reminiscent of markings on a Gadwall or female wigeon.

PUNA TINAMOU (*Tinamotis pentlandii*) is found in a variety of high-altitude habitats, from the edges of bogs to desert-like puna. These birds are shy and hard to see well—although in areas such as the high plains south of Uyuni, Bolivia, they can sometimes be seen scurrying between the few isolated clumps of low shrubs found in the region. This large tinamou has a striped head, reminiscent of a young grebe, and a rufous belly, both of which are distinctive field marks. This species is seen in groups more often than many other species of tinamou, and the males take care of the young, as is the case with other members of the family Tinamidae.

CREAMY-BREASTED CANASTERO (*Asthenes dorbignyi*) is a typical skulking, long-tailed furnariid that is widely distributed in the altiplano from Peru to Chile. It prefers hiding in the spiky leaves at the base of Puya bromeliads and is subtly plumaged but beautiful—with orange throat patches and tan and gray coloration. This picture shows the "Rusty-vented" subspecies and was taken in the highlands southeast of Cochabamba in Bolivia.

WHITE-TUFTED GREBE (*Rollandia rolland*) is a small but distinctive member of its genus. Reminiscent of an Eared Grebe, this species can be found along the Peruvian coast and on higher-altitude lakes, including those around Cochabamba, Bolivia, where this picture was taken. It ranges from the Andes and coasts of Peru to the lowlands of Brazil and Argentina.

PUNA MINER (*Geositta punensis*) is similar in appearance to the Common Miner but has a plain, rather than streaked, breast. It is found from southern Peru through Bolivia into Argentina; this individual was photographed close to Laguna Hedionda, in the altiplano of Bolivia. Puna Miners spend most of their time foraging on what appears to be barren puna and show a bright cinnamon-buff wing bar when they fly.

The ubiquitous **RUFOUS-COLLARED SPARROW** (*Zonotrichia capensis*) is often the first bird seen or heard on any trip to the Andes. It is found in a variety of habitats, usually in more open areas, including around towns and cities. Like many common species, it is easy to overlook how striking and subtly beautiful this familiar species is.

ANDEAN FLICKER

(*Colaptes rupicola*) is a spectacular and frequently encountered resident of high-altitude open areas, occurring from Ecuador to Chile. When this appealing woodpecker is viewed feeding on the ground or perching on a disused adobe building, its bright buff underparts, barred upperparts, and typical flicker countenance make it nearly unmistakable.

PUNA PLOVER (*Anarhynchus alticola*) is the only small plover likely to be encountered in the highlands, where it can be found foraging along the shores of lakes in the altiplano. It is a typical plover with a black mark at the side of the breast (adult), reminiscent of a Snowy Plover, but it also has a faint grayish-brown lower breast band. It is found from Peru to Chile in appropriate habitat within the puna and altiplano.

ANDEAN FLAMINGO (*Phoenicoparrus andinus*) is the least common of the three high Andean flamingo species. The Andean can be most easily separated by its yellow legs and by bill and face patterns. While the Chilean Flamingo is more widespread, the Andean and James's Flamingos are primarily confined to high-altitude saline lakes in Bolivia, Chile, and Argentina—although Andeans are sometimes found further afield outside the breeding season. These birds all perform spectacular displays in which they form large groups and twist their heads in unison; the precise timing of these displays, however, can vary depending on weather conditions.

ROSY-BILLED POCHARD (*Netta peposaca*) is a striking and, in the case of the male, unmistakable species that is primarily found in the southern part of South America. It is a partial austral migrant, and this seems to have led to the establishment of a resident breeding population in the Cochabamba Basin of Bolivia, where this photograph was taken. This species, like several other waterfowl, practices nest parasitism—although it is not an obligate parasite like the Black-headed Duck, another Southern Cone species.

THE EAST SLOPE 4

THE EAST SLOPE of the Andes is most pronounced as a topographic feature in Ecuador, Peru, and eastern Bolivia, since the multiple cordilleras of the Colombian Andes create a different geologic and biogeographic profile. In Ecuador and Peru in particular, the East Slope tends to be a more singular feature, since the Andes mostly span only a single distinct cordillera in these countries (albeit with a central "inter-Andean" region in some areas), although they are generally wider in Peru than they are in Ecuador. Technically, however, the "east slope" is any slope that ultimately drains into the Amazon River. For the purposes of this book, we will focus primarily on the often steep slopes that are covered with dense Andean Cloud Forest and are found from approximately Cayambe-Coca National Park in central northern Ecuador to Madidi National Park in northern Bolivia, as well as along the eastern slope of the Colombian Cordillera Oriental. We also include the Amazonian lowlands, which essentially begin at the base of the Andes Mountains on their eastern flank, and the dry southeastern foothills, which have a more xeric character and their own suite of birds.

The East Slope includes at least five Endemic Bird Areas, each with its own clusters of restricted-range species, so the East Slope is by no means a homogeneous system; some birds, such as the Royal Sunangel, Pale-billed Antpitta, and Hooded Mountain-Toucan, occupy only small areas along the slope. This section therefore looks at several of the main habitats and ecoregions of the East Slope, including cloud and yungas forest, the drier foothills of the southeast, and the eastern flank of Amazonia.

BLUE-GRAY TANAGER (*Thraupis episcopus*) is a common, widespread, and variable species found in lowland and foothill forests throughout the Andean region and beyond. Subtle plumage differences separate this species from the northern Glaucous Tanager and the superficially similar Sayaca Tanager, which comes close to overlapping the present species' range in the eastern Andes of Bolivia—but the Blue-gray Tanagers there have white wing bars, which are lacking in Sayaca Tanagers. An introduced population of Blue-gray Tanagers in Lima, Peru, consists of both white-winged and non-white-winged birds.

CLOUD FOREST

COLLARED INCA (*Coeligena torquata*) is one of the most dramatically patterned of all hummingbirds, and one of the most instantly recognizable. It is found throughout the Andes, from Venezuela to north-central Bolivia, at altitudes up to about 10,000 feet. Southern populations (from roughly Cusco, Peru, to central Bolivia), where both sexes show an orange, rather than a white, breast, are now often split and known as Gould's Inca.

CLOUD FOREST — BIOGEOGRAPHY AND HISTORY

The East Slope often feels like the core of the core when it comes to bird diversity. These forests are humid, rich in biodiversity, and varied in topography and elevation, and they provide the ideal conditions for some of the greatest bird diversity on Earth. The trees are often covered in mosses and bromeliads, and clumps of bamboo can frequently be found in the understory. Trees are usually shorter than in lowland rain forest and have branches that grow closer to the ground. There is also usually a subcanopy as well as dense undergrowth—which makes these forests hard to penetrate away from trails. While the East Slope is a continuum that ranges from snow-capped peaks, through the páramo at its high edge, to humid lowland forest on its lower extremity, it is the cloud forest that forms the beating heart of this most amazing of Earth's ecosystems. In fact, Madidi National Park, Bolivia, is known as the protected area with the most bird species of any equivalent area on the planet. Manu National Park, Peru, is surely not far behind, and the famed Manu Road is a classic birding route; bird tours that go there often run up huge totals of species. More off the regular beaten birding path, areas such as Chingaza National Natural Park in Colombia and its environs also offer great East Slope birding, as well as rare endemics, such as the Cundinamarca Antpitta that Peter Kaestner discovered near Refugio del Tororoi in 1989.

Cloud forests contain myriad subhabitats depending on how one wants to define the differences between each type, and these can include lichen- and moss-rich elfin forests, bamboo forests, and a variety of wetter and drier forest types (biologists sometimes separate them into Andean Cloud Forest, Temperate Cloud Forest, and Elfin Forest). One of the reasons that these areas have so many species is that the varying altitudes and microhabitats of the East Slope life zone offer so many different niches for specialized species to exploit. One major division that is often referred to is the difference between classic Andean Cloud Forest and yungas forest. The latter is found from extreme southeastern Peru, through Bolivia, to northern Argentina. It tends to be somewhat drier, is found in cooler areas, has a more broken canopy and smaller-leaved undergrowth plants, and often has trees that are semievergreen. Above both yungas and montane cloud forest, some areas have patches of elfin forest, which usually has a spongy ground cover of lichens and mosses and whose tree species tend to be similar to those in the cloud forest below but are stunted. Several bird species have a particular affinity for these areas, including the Bar-winged Wood-Wren and Royal Sunangel. Depending on the degree of humidity in the forest and the altitude, yungas forest itself is also sometimes divided into Humid Yungas, Semi-Evergreen Yungas, Dry Deciduous Yungas, and High Yungas.

A feature of all these steep, forested slopes is frequent landslides, some of which affect large areas of habitat. Their effect can often be seen from a distance on clear days. These landslides act to create habitat disturbance and forest renewal, and some bird species, such as Johnson's Tody-Flycatcher, appear to depend on them.

Historically, these cloud forest areas were part of the Incan Empire, which has been referred to several times elsewhere in this book. In northern Peru, the Chachapoyas culture also inhabited cloud forest and associated habitats. There is evidence that areas that were once centers for the development of early human civilization are also the epicenters of biological diversity hotspots. In fact, it is thought that in some cases, the exact conditions that foster human cultural development—a stable climate, a reliable source of water, and the availability of food—also give rise to the evolution of the most abundant and unique biological diversity.

VIOLET-FRONTED BRILLIANT (*Heliodoxa leadbeateri*) is the East Slope version of the familiar Green-crowned Brilliant of the Chocó and western slope (female pictured). This aptly named, large hummingbird is found from Venezuela to Bolivia in mid-altitude and foothill forests at elevations up to about 7,000 feet. A good place to see this species is the Copalinga Reserve, in southern Ecuador, managed by Fundación Jocotoco.

BIRD DIVERSITY AND SPECIALTIES — CLOUD FOREST

The overall avifauna of the East Slope is basically mind-blowing. The diversity of spectacular tropical families and species is staggering. These include mountain tanagers and mountain-toucans in the upper reaches of the cloud forest; large mixed flocks of colorful tanagers moving through the canopy in the company of funariids and other flocking species in the mid-elevations; and Magpie, Palm, and Blue-gray Tanagers, along with other more low elevation-associated species as you travel downslope through the Andean Cloud Forest to East Andean Foothill Forest. In many cases, the east and west slopes of the Andes have unique forms of widespread species—the racket-tailed hummingbirds, for example, which have white "boots" in the west and cinnamon-colored "boots" in the east. Some of these forms are split as separate species and some are not, and sometimes it depends on whose taxonomy you are using. There are also species like the Andean Cock-of-the-rock that are found on both slopes but lack obvious morphological differences and are actually more different between their northern and southern populations than they are between eastern and western groups. There are even species like the Collared Inca, which differs both north to south *and* east to west. One major biogeographic obstacle to gene flow in the region is the Marañón Valley of northern Peru, which often creates a line of separation between subspecies or species. While this is probably the most dramatic example of this phenomenon, the incredibly varied topography of the region means that this is by no means a unique circumstance.

The East Slope cloud forests are particularly known from a birding standpoint for the amazing mixed-species flocks that can be encountered there from time to time. Keeping up with the action when you find yourself in the midst of one of these flocks can be daunting. Often there are two associated flocks, a canopy flock and an understory flock, making the birding both extremely fun and extremely challenging at the same time. Some common East Slope birds include the ubiquitous Gray-breasted Wood-Wren, Great Thrush, Pearled Treerunner, and Barred Becard, as well as brushfinches, conebills, barbets, flowerpiercers, antpittas, fruiteaters, tapaculos, woodcreepers and other furnariids (the elegant Streaked Tuftedcheek, for example), euphonias, many species of hummingbird, various species of tyrannulet, and also several neotropical migrants—especially Blackburnian Warblers and Swainson's Thrushes. There are hundreds of species in total, often moving in mixed flocks—with species suites that can change considerably during a few miles' drive either up- or downslope. The Bolivian yungas also hold Black-hooded Sunbeams, Hooded Mountain-Toucans, and other unique species that birders should not overlook.

WHITE-WINGED BRUSHFINCH (*Atlapetes leucopterus*) has a relatively limited distribution, ranging from northern Ecuador south to Peru (north of the Marañón Valley). It overlaps with the similar Bay-crowned Brushfinch in southern Ecuador and northern Peru, but that species lacks the white wing patch. White-winged is geographically variable, and its taxonomy might not be fully resolved. For example, the distinctive white-crowned "Paynter's" subspecies of southern Ecuador may be a valid but currently unrecognized species.

CLOUD FOREST > CONSERVATION

The cloud forest of the East Slope benefits from large protected areas and overall is in relatively good condition in comparison to the inter-Andean valleys or, for example, the eastern Brazilian Amazon. So, fortunately, there are relatively fewer highly endangered bird species in this region. Those that do qualify as among the most endangered tend to have extremely limited altitudinal and geographic ranges, such as the Golden-backed Mountain Tanager and Jocotoco Antpitta, both classified as Endangered, and the Vulnerable Long-whiskered Owlet.

There are a number of very large government-managed protected areas in this habitat. In addition, conservation organizations manage an increasing number of smaller reserves that are designed to augment the larger reserves by adding areas of habitat that are needed by endangered species but are not covered by the government-managed areas. Two such sites that stand out—both supported by American Bird Conservancy—are the Tapichalaca Reserve in southern Ecuador and Abra Patricia in northern Peru, each of which protects significant acreage of Temperate Cloud Forest.

Tapichalaca, which lies on the southern border of Podocarpus National Park, was founded after ornithologist Robert Ridgely discovered a distinctive and previously undescribed species of antpitta there in 1997. The species was named Jocotoco Antpitta based on an onomatopoeic name used by local people. Tapichalaca then became the flagship reserve for the Ecuadorian conservation group Fundación Jocotoco (fittingly named after the Jocotoco Antpitta found by Dr. Ridgely), which has since expanded and added fourteen additional reserves throughout Ecuador. Abra Patricia was established in the early 2000s by the Peruvian conservation organization ECOAN (Asociación Ecosistemas Andinos). The reserve was designed to augment the Alto Mayo Protection Forest by adding critical highland habitat not included in the official protected area. The reserve essentially conserves the top of the Alto Mayo watershed and includes elfin forest as well as cloud forest. It was originally intended to protect the only known population of the Long-whiskered Owlet, although the owlet has subsequently been found at nearby sites. Nevertheless, Abra Patricia is still vitally important for this species as well as for such birds as the Cinnamon Screech-Owl, Bar-winged Wood-Wren, Ochre-fronted Antpitta, Johnson's Tody-Flycatcher, Yellow-scarfed Tanager, Royal Sunangel, and many more. The lodge's hummingbird feeders and gardens also attract species such as Sword-billed Hummingbird, Chestnut-breasted Coronet, and Emerald-bellied Puffleg. The Abra Patricia Reserve also provided ECOAN with a staging post to expand conservation in the region. For example, it has helped the organization add a small protected area and lodge at Huembo, one of the critical sites for the spectacular Marvelous Spatuletail, which is one of the must-see birds of the East Slope and, really, of the entire planet. The spatuletails can be seen coming to feeders close to the lodge and also, potentially, at a lek across the road from the reserve. Their lek is truly one of the most amazing bird spectacles anywhere, as the males compete for supremacy while raising their tail spatules and moving back and forth while hovering.

The reserve has also provided a base of operations for ECOAN to protect a large nearby conservation concession, and to develop a program supported by Conservation International to help reduce deforestation in the Alto Mayo Forest on the lower slopes below the reserve. ECOAN has also since worked with local communities to designate additional reserves on community lands in the area for species such as the Pale-billed Antpitta. The Abra Patricia Reserve was made possible thanks to the support of the Gordon and Betty Moore Foundation through American Bird Conservancy; the foresight of Adrian Forsyth and Enrique Ortiz, who helped support the project; and the efforts of ECOAN's president, Constantino Aucca Chutas, who led the conservation work on the ground. There are many wonderful East Slope conservation sites, such as Wayqecha and other locations along the Manu Road in Peru, as well as a newly created conservation area for the Cundinamarca Antpitta in Colombia, to name just two. eBird hotspots in the region can help identify additional specific lodges that are suitable for a visit.

JOCOTOCO ANTPITTA (*Grallaria ridgelyi*) was discovered in 1997 by Dr. Robert Ridgely at what has since become Fundación Jocotoco's flagship reserve at Tapichalaca, in southeastern Ecuador. The species was subsequently also found in northern Peru, but after specimens were collected there, it has not been reported since. The species prefers cloud forest with bamboo thickets close to small streams and is found from roughly 7,500 to 8,500 feet in altitude.

BIRDING AND PHOTOGRAPHY SITES — CLOUD FOREST

The East Slope has a myriad of opportunities to build an amazing bird list and capture great photos. One classic trip is to leave Cusco, Peru, and drive down the Manu Road to Atalaya, stopping at various lodges along the way, then taking a boat on to the Manu Wildlife Center and Puerto Maldanado for lowland forest birding. A relatively new lodge at Villa Carmen managed by the Amazon Conservation Association is now a virtual must-stop location along this route. The road includes a lodge with access to an Andean Cock-of-the-rock lek site, and hundreds of species can potentially be found along the drive. On one trip I undertook, a Sunbittern wandered out onto the road in front of us and posed for photos until we had to leave.

Another great trip across the East Slope is in northern Peru, where the drive from Chiclayo to Tarapoto will take you through Tumbesian habitat, then through the deep canyon formed by the Marañón River to Abra Barro Negro, and on to Abra Patricia and points east (oilbirds can be seen along the road to Tarapoto from here). Similarly, it is possible to fly into Guayaquil, Ecuador, and traverse the East Slope while covering such key sites as Cerro de Arcos for the newly discovered Blue-throated Hillstar; then on to Buenaventura for birds such as El Oro Parakeet, Long-wattled Umbrellabird, and Club-winged Manakin; and finally to Tapichalaca (just east of the Continental Divide) for the famous Jocotoco Antpitta, and Copalinga for a variety of more eastern lowland-associated species, such as Gray Tinamou, Swallow Tanager, and Paradise Tanager. Many other such epic adventures await the enterprising birder, including, potentially, Madidi National Park, Bolivia, and through central Peru to the Oilbird cave at Tingo Maria National Park. Always be sure to check with your government's online resources for visitor safety, since the security situation in some of these areas can be somewhat fluid. This is typically not a reason not to go, however; your tour company or local guide will be able to advise on the best route for your trip.

SUNBITTERN (*Eurypyga helias*) is a distinctive species that is widespread in the neotropics. It has a greater affinity with the Amazonian lowlands than the Andes per se, but it is also found in the foothills and mid-elevations on both slopes—for example, near Mindo, Ecuador, and along the Manu Road, in Peru. These birds are among the most intricately patterned of all Andean birds, and their defensive display—in which they spread their boldly marked wings—is one of the great birding sights of the region. Sunbitterns can at times be extremely confiding, as long you are patient.

FORK-TAILED WOODNYMPH (*Thalurania furcata*) is an East Slope and Amazonian counterpart to the Crowned Woodnymph and is found at altitudes up to about 4,500 feet. The male has an iridescent green throat and breast and dark violet belly. The similar Crowned Woodnymph is found at higher altitudes and generally to the north and west of this species.

CRIMSON-CRESTED WOODPECKER (*Campephilus melanoleucos*) is one member of a group of nine remaining spectacular woodpecker species in a genus that once included the North American Ivory-billed and Imperial Woodpeckers (prior to their extinction). Despite the loss of these two species, many of the remaining birds, like the Crimson-crested Woodpecker, are widespread and common in the right habitat. This species is found widely in Colombia, through the eastern Andes of Ecuador and Peru, and into Amazonia—where its range extends south to Paraguay.

EQUATORIAL ANTPITTA (*Grallaria saturata*) is a small, mostly chestnut-colored antpitta that was split from the larger Rufous Antpitta group in 2020 based primarily on call differences. The Equatorial Antpitta ranges from Colombia to northern Peru in upper-elevation cloud forest, often with *Chusquea* bamboo thickets. Like most antpittas, these charismatic birds stick to the forest floor and undergrowth and are typically extremely difficult to see unless they happen to cross a trail. This species has, in recent years, become habituated to feeding at Zuroloma, in Ecuador, making this location a great place to try to see one.

CHESTNUT-NAPED ANTPITTA (*Grallaria nuchalis*) is a large, distinctive antpitta with gray underparts, brown upperparts, and a white eye ring. It is distributed in a relatively narrow altitudinal belt from about 6,000 to 9,000 feet in Colombia, Ecuador, and Peru, and it favors temperate cloud forest with dense stands of *Chusquea* bamboo. Despite its limited range, it is considered stable and is not listed as globally threatened. Birds in northwestern Ecuador—like the one pictured—have the bright chestnut mostly confined to the nape, whereas eastern-slope birds have bright rufous extending onto the crown. Like most antpittas, this species was historically difficult to find and photograph, but recent developments in birding tourism, including antpitta-feeding stations (particularly at Zuroloma, in northwestern Ecuador, and Tapichalaca, in southern Ecuador), have made it more feasible to see and photograph this and other antpitta species.

BLUE-CAPPED TANAGER (*Sporathraupis cyanocephala*) is found throughout the tropical Andes, from Venezuela to Bolivia. It is a commonly seen, conspicuous species primarily found at altitudes between 6,500 and 10,000 feet on both the eastern and western slopes, although it can sometimes be found as low as 1,100 feet. The most northeasterly populations (outside the Andes) have completely blue underparts, but those found in most of Colombia, in areas including the popular birding sites near Mindo, Ecuador, and farther south into Peru, have a grayish breast and belly. These birds often forage for berries and insects in the canopy of humid cloud forest and second-growth forest, including in *Cecropia* trees.

SLATE-THROATED REDSTART (*Myioborus miniatus*) is part of the family Parulidae, the New World wood warblers, and along with seven other closely related Andean species, is sometimes referred to as a "whitestart" because of its white outer tail feathers. In terms of North American relatives, the species is closest to the Painted Redstart, and it is not as closely related to the American Redstart, which is part of the genus *Setophaga*, rather than *Myioborus*. Attractive, animated Slate-throated Redstarts are often seen in mixed flocks foraging on dead leaf clusters or along branches at altitudes from about 2,000 feet up to about 10,000 feet. They reportedly move into the upper levels of this elevation zone when migrant warblers from North America are not present there.

YELLOW-BREASTED BRUSHFINCH (*Atlapetes latinuchus*) ranges from Venezuela to central Peru, being found on both slopes at altitudes up to about 12,000 feet. The species can skulk but does come to feeders at times—for example, at Zuroloma, in Ecuador—and it is generally more conspicuous than other brushfinches. Some populations show a small white wing patch, but all have yellow underparts and a rufous crown. The similar Tricolored Brushfinch is generally found at lower altitudes and has a paler crown.

GOLDEN-TAILED SAPPHIRE (*Chrysuronia oenone*) is found in the foothills and lowlands of the East Slope at altitudes up to about 5,500 feet. In the right light, these small hummingbirds are absolutely stunning, with their blue head (or crown, depending on the subspecies) and bronze-to-rufous-to-gold rump and tail. They are usually encountered in more open areas and along forest edge and may attend feeders in some locations.

MASKED TROGON (*Trogon personatus*) is a widespread species that ranges from Venezuela to Brazil and Bolivia at a range of altitudes from about 3,000 feet to nearly 10,000 feet. The blotchy black-and-white undertail of the male helps to separate Masked from the similar Collared Trogon, which has a generally paler and more broadly barred undertail pattern. These birds often sit still for long periods and are usually best located by their call.

SAPPHIRE-VENTED PUFFLEG (*Eriocnemis luciani*) is found at altitudes above about 8,800 feet along the main spine of the Andes, from extreme southern Colombia to eastern and southern Peru. It is found in the central Andes of Ecuador, but only on the East Slope in Peru. This species is the largest of the pufflegs, and while its different populations have plumage variations, all populations (and both sexes) have prominent white leg puffs as well as a forked tail with violet or blue undertail coverts. This puffleg is mostly associated with forest openings and forest-edge habitats.

GRAY-BREASTED SABREWING (*Campylopterus largipennis*) is a large, rather nondescript hummingbird found from Amazonia up to about 4,000 feet in the Andean foothills. It is fairly widely distributed along the East Slope and into eastern and northern Amazonia. This species' prominent white tail tips are a good clue to its identity, as are the silky-looking gray underparts. Gray-breasted Sabrewings are associated with open areas and secondary habitats and frequently attend hummingbird feeders at Waqanki, near Moyobamba, Peru, which is a great place to see them—along with a variety of other hummingbirds and eastern-foothill forest species.

PERUVIAN RACKET-TAIL (*Ocreatus peruanus*) is a sister species to the White-booted Racket-tail of Venezuela, Colombia, and Ecuador. While generally found to the south of the White-booted, it also occurs on the East Slope of the Andes in Ecuador and southern Colombia. This subspecies is also found to the north of the more southerly distributed Rufous-booted Racket-tail, which has twisted, rather than straight, tail feathers. All three birds are tiny, spectacular, and among the most unusual and charismatic of all hummingbirds.

ORNATE FLYCATCHER (*Myiotriccus ornatus*) is found commonly on both slopes of the Andes and ranges from Colombia to Peru. These distinctive, small flycatchers are usually found singly or in pairs well below the canopy on lower branches, and they occur at altitudes up to about 7,500 feet. Like many flycatchers, they habitually return to the same perch and can be confiding, if you are patient. They are usually found in humid primary forest, along forest edge, or in older secondary forest.

SWAINSON'S THRUSH (*Catharus ustulatus*) is one of the most obvious North American-breeding migrants in the Andes. It occurs in a range of habitats up to mid-elevations, and it ranges south to northern Argentina in a variety of forested and disturbed habitats. Swainson's Thrushes are present throughout the region from about October to April and will attend moth feeders along with resident woodcreepers, trogons, and warblers.

CINNAMON SCREECH-OWL (*Megascops petersoni*) has a narrow and patchily-known distributional range from Venezuela to northern Peru. It is generally not a well-known species but can be reliably seen at ECOAN's Abra Patricia Reserve, in northern Peru. Like most forest owls, it is most easily found and identified by its voice.

SCALY-NAPED PARROT (*Amazona mercenarius*) is the only *Amazona* parrot found in the high Andes, where it occurs at altitudes up to 11,000 feet. These parrots range from Venezuela to Bolivia and look almost entirely green when perched, but they have red in the outer secondaries and outer tail feathers—which is most easily visible in flight. As with most *Amazona* parrots, their wingbeats are shallow and rapid, and this, as well as the calls, can help to separate them from other parrots found at mid- to upper elevations (such as the Red-billed Parrot) when seen from a distance.

COLLARED TROGON (*Trogon collaris*) is widely distributed throughout the Andes of Colombia and Ecuador and along the East Slope of Peru into Amazonia, generally at altitudes below about 4,000 feet. While similar to the Masked Trogon, the Collared Trogon occurs at lower elevations, and the undertail barring of Collared is wider in the male and more diffuse in the female than it is on Masked.

FAWN-BREASTED BRILLIANT (*Heliodoxa rubinoides*) is found throughout the three cordilleras of the Colombian Andes at altitudes up to about 8,500 feet and ranges south through Ecuador to central Peru, with records as far south as the Cochabamba area of Bolivia. The sexes are overall similar, although males have a larger pink throat patch. These elegant hummingbirds are frequent visitors to feeders and can easily be seen in the Mindo area of Ecuador, for example.

EMERALD-BELLIED PUFFLEG (*Eriocnemis aline*) is restricted to a narrow altitudinal range in the upper cloud forests of the Andes from Colombia to northern Peru. Fortunately, though, this tiny sparkling gem of a hummingbird is not considered to be threatened with extinction, and the Abra Patricia Reserve, in northern Peru, is a great place to see it.

CHESTNUT-BREASTED CORONET (*Boissonneaua matthewsii*) is a familiar bird of the higher Andean cloud forests, where it is mostly found on the East Slope above 6,000 feet in altitude from southern Colombia to Peru (although narrowly more to the west in southern Ecuador). These boisterous hummingbirds are often found at feeders and try to boss the other hummingbirds around. This is one of the most numerous hummingbirds at ECOAN's Abra Patricia Reserve, in northern Peru, which is a great place to see the species.

LESSER VIOLETEAR (*Colibri cyanotus*) is similar to the Sparkling Violetear but lacks the blue belly and white-tipped undertail coverts of that species, and Lesser has a green (not violet) chin and upper throat. It is found from southern Central America to Bolivia, with a South American range that is strongly tied to the Andean mountain chain. Like some other species, it is more widespread in Colombia and mostly restricted to the East Slope to the south in Peru.

BLACKBURNIAN WARBLER (*Setophaga fusca*) is a migratory neotropical species that has a strong wintering affinity for the Andes. It is found from Colombia to Bolivia and east to Brazil during the nonbreeding season. Along with the Swainson's Thrush, this is probably the northern migrant encountered most commonly in most Andean forests. It is also often seen in secondary growth, where it tends to forage in the canopy as part of a mixed-species flock.

WHITE-THROATED SCREECH-OWL

(*Megascops albogularis*) is a relatively widespread, medium-sized owl whose distribution mirrors that of many Andean birds: ranging from Venezuela in the north, distributed fairly widely in Colombia and Ecuador, limited mostly to the more humid East Slope in Peru, and then reaching into Bolivia at its southern extreme. While primarily nocturnal, this species has been coming to a feeder at Zuroloma, in Ecuador, during the day.

LONG-TAILED SYLPH

(*Aglaiocercus kingii*) is the East Slope and higher-altitude equivalent of the Violet-tailed Sylph (which is commonly found at lower elevations in the west, for example, in northwestern Ecuador). Long-tailed has a bluer sheen on the tail than the similar Violet-tailed, and the males also lack the violet-blue throat patch of that species—which is blue-green instead. Females have a green, rather than blue, crown and lack the white breast shown by Violet-tailed.

RED-CRESTED COTINGA (*Ampelion rubrocristatus*) is found throughout the Andes from Venezuela to Bolivia at altitudes above about 7,000 feet. It is found in both primary forest and more disturbed areas. Although this species appears to be mainly gray, its red crest and white tail markings make it a dapper and striking bird when seen well. Because these cotingas often sit still on a prominent perch for a lengthy period, it can be possible to set up a telescope to get a better view of one on an exposed branch on a nearby forested ridgeline.

CHESTNUT-CROWNED ANTPITTA (*Grallaria ruficapilla*) is typical of the forest antpittas in that it skulks and is hard to see well. This species is, however, one of the more numerous and widespread of the antpittas, and (other than the Tawny Antpitta, which likes more open habitats) it is perhaps the antpitta that you are most likely to encounter in regular field conditions away from feeders. It is found from Venezuela through all three ranges of the Colombian Andes to central Peru, up to about 9,000 feet.

STRONG-BILLED WOODCREEPER

(*Xiphocolaptes promeropirhynchus*) is a widely but patchily distributed species found from Mexico to Bolivia along the Andean chain and east into Amazonia. It occurs at altitudes ranging from a few hundred feet to nearly 10,000 feet. This species is adaptable in terms of its feeding strategy and can forage on trunks or bromeliads, or it can follow army-ant swarms to feed on insects that the ants disturb or attack. It has a long, thick, black bill and is generally large and robust. In the field, it often is wise to try to capture a photograph to confirm its identity, since several species are superficially similar to this woodcreeper within its range. These birds often attend the moth feeders at the Birdwatcher's House, near Mindo, Ecuador, which is a great place to see them, along with many other species.

BLUE-NECKED TANAGER (*Stilpnia cyanicollis*) is a stunning typical tanager with a broad distribution in open habitats on both Andean slopes and into the lowlands, from Venezuela to Bolivia, with a separate population in central Brazil. Western birds have a blue rump, and those in the east have a yellowish rump. Along with such birds as the Paradise Tanager, this is one of the species most likely to elicit a "Wow!" from birders putting their binoculars on one for the first (or even tenth) time.

The magnificent **SWORD-BILLED HUMMINGBIRD** (*Ensifera ensifera*) is one of the most unusual and spectacular birds in the world: its bill is virtually as long as the rest of the body. It is found at mid- to upper elevations on both slopes of the Andes, from Venezuela to Bolivia. It is a large species whose distinctive, loud *chip* flight call often announces its appearance at feeders. Sword-billed Hummingbirds often perch with their bill raised and seldom remain long at feeders. Their natural food plants include passion flowers in the genus *Passiflora*, which they tend to visit in a predictable pattern. They can be readily seen at sites like Zuroloma, in Ecuador, and at Abra Patricia, in Peru.

ORANGE-BILLED SPARROW (*Arremon aurantiirostris*) is a striking and attractive bird of the forest floor. It is found in the lowlands at altitudes up to about 3,000 feet from southern Mexico to Peru. The bird is aptly named, as it is often the brightly colored bill that is the first thing that you notice about the species—and the sparrow is most often seen in poorly lit areas through the undergrowth. Orange-billed Sparrows skulk less and are more easily seen than many other forest-floor species.

GREAT PAMPA-FINCH (*Embernagra platensis*) is a large, distinctive finch that is found in open areas, including in the highlands of Bolivia and Argentina, as well as in the lowlands and marshes of Brazil and Uruguay. This is a species that appears to benefit from deforestation, as it has, for example, recently expanded east of Santa Cruz, Bolivia, into agricultural areas.

RED-AND-GREEN and BLUE-AND-YELLOW MACAWS (*Ara chloropterus* and *A. ararauna*) attend a clay lick close to Tambopata Research Station in the Peruvian Amazon. The Station is managed by the innovative ecotourism company Rainforest Expeditions, and lies within the Tambopata National Reserve.

AMAZONIA > BIOGEOGRAPHY AND HISTORY

It would be reasonable to argue that a section on Amazonia does not belong in a book about the Andes. However, Amazonia depends completely on the Andes, and the mountains and lowlands are inexorably connected both biologically and hydrologically. Without the Andes, there is no Amazon—at least not as we know it. The Amazon River originates in the Andes, and the region's weather systems are integrally connected and intertwined. Its inclusion here also makes sense from a birding point of view, since if you are traveling to the region from outside of South America, it makes a lot of sense to divide your time between the highlands and the lowlands to see the greatest diversity of species.

Amazonia as a whole needs little general introduction in a book for nature and conservation enthusiasts. It is replete with superlatives, and perhaps most importantly, it is the largest contiguous block of tropical forest on planet Earth. As the foothills of the eastern slope of the Andes peter out in southeastern Colombia, eastern Ecuador and Peru, and northern—and especially northeastern—Bolivia, the landscape becomes cloaked in a deep, uninterrupted layer of tall rain forest trees that are usually broken only by the

BRAZILIAN TEAL (*Amazonetta brasiliensis*) is a relatively nondescript duck of the lowlands—that is, until it takes flight and its stunning iridescent blue-and-white pattern becomes visible. Brazilian Teal range from northern Argentina through central Brazil and have spread along the edge of the Andes to Peru, Ecuador, and through Colombia, perhaps aided by deforestation in the region. They can be found on lakes and marshes and in rice paddies.

large meandering rivers and oxbow lakes that are found across the region. Unfortunately, these forests are increasingly also disturbed by clearings for timber extraction, agriculture, and pasture, especially around the larger towns, such as Iquitos and Puerto Maldanado in Peru. Oil and gas extraction is also leading to forest clearance—for example, in Ecuador and Peru—and represents a significant and growing threat to habitat in the region.

Within the forest itself, common large trees include Brazil nut trees, Ceibas, ironwoods, palms, *Ingas*, cedars, rubber trees, mahogany, magnolias, fig trees, and cacao. While there are thousands of tree species in total, the majority of Amazonian trees belong to just a couple of hundred species. The region is known for the size of its evergreen trees, which average about a hundred feet or more in height.

There is also a multiplicity of forest types across Amazonia, but perhaps the most important from a bird and biodiversity point of view are Terra Firme Forest (ground remains dry all year) and Várzea and Igapo Forest (seasonally flooded forest). Terra Firme tends to be dominated by the aforementioned trees, but Várzea—at least the areas closest to rivers—is most often characterized by stands of *Cecropia*, moriche palms, and bamboo forest. Depending on location, these forest types tend to support different bird communities. Other important types include White Sand Forest—literally, forest growing on white sand areas. While these areas may have originated from river beaches, scientists aren't yet completely certain how they formed. There is also permanently flooded forest and other areas that are dominated by palms and lianas. The Amazon has distinct seasons. The wet season takes place from about November to April, and most of the rain forest's rain falls during this period. During this season, the major rivers are often in flood and carry huge amounts of sediment from the Andes into the floodplain of the Amazon and beyond.

One major biological feature of Amazonian forest that is important to birds is the presence of army-ant swarms. While some army ants appear in other ecosystems, it is in the lowlands (for example, Amazonia and the Chocó) where the true "antbirds" are primarily found—those that depend completely on army-ant swarms for their food. The birds do not eat the ants themselves but forage around the swarm, picking off larger insects that are fleeing the ant swarm or have been killed or maimed by the ants. Some Amazonian antbirds that are swarm obligates include the Black-spotted Bare-eye, Hairy-crested Antbird, and White-cheeked Antbird. In the Chocó, Bicolored and Ocellated Antbirds also tend to be swarm obligates.

Amazonia contains more than three thousand acknowledged indigenous people's territories, and about 2.5 million indigenous people currently live in the region, but, tragically, they have been decimated by introduced diseases or had their cultures and lands disrupted and/or appropriated by colonial powers. Despite this, about sixty indigenous groups in the region remain largely uncontacted by contemporary society. Protected areas designed to preserve the rights of indigenous communities began to be established in the early 1960s, and conservation groups have hailed these areas as successes. However, in many cases, the story is similar to that of indigenous cultures elsewhere in the world—the first people have been largely marginalized and driven from much of their ancestral lands by later colonists. Threats to the Amazon continue to this day, and the conservation of the area remains both a global conservation imperative and a huge challenge.

AMAZONIA > BIRD DIVERSITY AND SPECIALTIES

Amazonia as a whole hosts more than a thousand bird species, and these can be grouped according to habitat—for example, whether they are species connected to rivers (such as kingfishers, swallows, and herons), to Várzea Forest (such as Ash-breasted Antbird, Varzea Shiffornis, and Wattled Curassow), or to Terra Firme Forest (such as many antbirds, parrots, and curassows). Some species also move between life zones. For example, some parrots may use clay licks along rivers but nest in larger trees farther from the water. Additional species can be found in disturbed areas, where land is cleared for agriculture, and yet others are ant-swarm followers.

No chapter on Amazonian birds would be complete without mention of macaws. Amazonia is a great place to see several of the largest and most spectacular macaws: Scarlet, Green-winged, and Blue-and-yellow. Some smaller macaw species can also be found, including Blue-headed, Chestnut-fronted, and Red-bellied. Other classic Amazonian birds include the distinctive Sungrebe; the primitive, leaf-eating Hoatzin; and the spectacular Harpy Eagle.

Along rivers—which is often the way most birders first gain access to Amazonian habitats—it is also possible to see such species as the Jabiru Stork, Large-billed Tern, roosting flocks of Sand-colored Nighthawks on islands; and, often, Bat Falcons and Swallow-winged Puffbirds, which can be seen perching on riverside trees. Migratory Buff-breasted and Pectoral Sandpipers can sometimes also be found on the exposed floodplains of the larger rivers, such as in the vicinity of Iquitos, Peru. Five kingfisher species in Amazonia are also commonly found along rivers, with the Green-and-rufous tending to be the least common, depending on location.

In the dense side streams of larger rivers, it is sometimes possible to find the spectacular Agami Heron, although the mysterious Zigzag Heron is among the toughest birds to find in these forests. Wild Muscovy Ducks are often found in the region's oxbow lakes. Piping-guans and Razor-billed Curassows can be sometimes be seen, especially in areas free from hunting, and even the enigmatic Nocturnal Curassow might be found—on the Napo River in Ecuador, for example. Other species occurring in these forests include forest-falcons, jacamars, King Vultures, nunbirds, toucans, aracaris, and a variety of parrot species, including *Amazona* and *Pionus* species, as well as many species of antshrikes, antbirds, some antthrushes, the amazing Long-billed Woodcreeper, cotingas and manakins, tityras, such tanagers as the Swallow Tanager and Guira Tanager, oropendolas, caciques, and many, many more.

Many Amazonian microhabitats also have specialized species that are restricted to them. For example, palm stands can provide habitat for Point-tailed Palmcreepers, while species such as the Varzea Schiffornis and Wattled Curassow are mostly restricted to Várzea Forest. Amazonia also provides important wintering and stopover habitat for several migratory neotropical birds, including, for example, Blackpoll Warblers, Scarlet Tanagers, Common Nighthawks, Purple Martins, Buff-breasted Sandpipers, Ospreys, and Eastern Kingbirds (which can be found roosting in large numbers in and around the town of Puerto Maldanado, Peru, during the northern winter).

HOATZIN (*Opisthocomus hoazin*) is a unique and truly unusual species that is strongly associated with oxbow lakes and slow-moving waterways. Almost always found in large groups, these strange prehistoric-looking birds have a unique gastric system designed to make the most of the leaves that form most of their diet. The young sometimes drop into the water to avoid predators, but their wings are equipped with small claws that enable the birds to clamber back into the low branches to avoid drowning. Hoatzins seem clumsy in flight and upon landing, often raising their wings as if to balance. The species is essentially confined to the Amazon Basin and the rivers that feed the Amazon flowing out of the Andes.

AMAZONIA > CONSERVATION

Because of its size and relative ecological homogeneity in comparison to the high Andes, western Amazonia has fewer highly threatened birds. It is also relatively less threatened than some other parts of Amazonia, although this is unlikely to last. Exceptions include species such as the Endangered Wattled Curassow and Critically Endangered Sira Curassow, which, in addition to having restricted ranges and habitats, are subject to hunting pressure. It also has fewer Endemic Bird Areas in relation to its area than other parts of the region (since the more varied topography of the Andes tends to lead to greater endemicity), and those that do exist tend to be focused around extremely specialized habitats, such as the Upper Amazon–Napo Lowlands Endemic Bird Area (selected for species such as Black-tailed Antbird) and the South-east Peruvian Lowlands Endemic Bird Area, to which such species as the Rufous-fronted Antthrush and Selva Cacique are restricted.

The conservation of Amazonian forests is a global priority, both for biodiversity conservation and to ensure that the vast amount of carbon stored in the region's forests remains in trees and is not released into the atmosphere. The majority of Amazonia lies far from the Andes, even though the influence of the mountains can be felt all the way to the mouth of the Amazon River and, indeed, beyond, as sediment is released into the Atlantic Ocean. In fact, it is possible for a drop of water to fall at Abra de Porculla in Peru, on the eastern edge of the Continental Divide, and then travel more than two thousand miles (measured in a straight line, or more than twice that distance by river) to the mouth of the Amazon River in northeastern Brazil.

The Amazon is currently under serious threat from deforestation driven by agricultural and pastoral expansion and mining—many would say it is fighting for its very survival. The most rapid loss of forest in recent years has taken place in the southeastern portion of the Amazon in Brazil. With new political leadership there starting in October 2022, this appears to be slowing, but the threat of land clearance remains. Scientists such as the great Thomas Lovejoy who have studied Amazonian ecology and fragmentation have warned of a tipping point where the Amazon's moisture cycle begins to break down after about 25 percent of the forest is lost. Under such conditions, almost certainly exacerbated by climate change, parts of the region would transition from forest to a much drier savanna habitat. This may already be happening in parts of the eastern Amazon, where deforestation has already exceeded 30 percent. Fortunately, the western Amazon closer to the Andes remains more intact; the most extensive loss in this area has taken place in south-central Colombia, central Peru, and southern Bolivia. Several large protected areas have been created in these countries to conserve what remains of the Amazon biome. The future of much more than Amazonia depends on their success, as well as on the expansion of conservation across larger areas of the region's forests.

AMAZONIAN MOTMOT (*Momotus momota*) is surely one of the most beautiful and exotic-looking birds of the tropical Andes, where it is found at altitudes up to about 3,000 feet on the East Slope. All motmots have a habit of moving their tails from side to side like a pendulum clock and make similar whooping calls. They frequently sit still on a low branch, and their tail movement (perhaps a predator response) and call can be the best clues to their presence.

BIRDING AND PHOTOGRAPHY SITES > AMAZONIA

Amazonia fortunately has many great birding sites. Most of these tend to be based around lodges on the major rivers, which are frequently best reached by boat from the region's larger towns. These include, for example: Sacha Lodge, La Selva, and the Napo Wildlife Center on the Napo River in Ecuador; and in Peru, Muyuna Lodge along the Amazon River itself near Iquitos, the Manu Wildlife Center along the Madre de Dios River; and Tambopata Research Center, Posada Amazonas (established by Rainforest Expeditions with the Ese Eja Infierno native community), and Explorer's Inn along the Tambopata River. Birding travel to such locations may feel at the outset more like an expedition than a regular birding trip, but most lodges have very comfortable accommodations and excellent trails and visitor facilities. Each location offers something a bit different, and the character of the forest and bird communities often changes between locations, so they are definitely not all the same when it comes to birding.

A spectacular feature that is worth going out of your way to witness is the parrot clay licks that are found on the Madre de Dios and Tambopata Rivers in Peru. Note that at the Tambopata Research Center, the Colorado lick blind allows photographers to approach closer than the main lick on the river. Parrots gather in large numbers at these licks to ingest minerals that counteract toxins in the plants they feed on.

You should expect the lowland Amazonian environment to be warm and humid (yet don't be surprised by the occasional seasonal blast of colder wind), and there are definitely biting insects to contend with, but these can vary seasonally and between locations. It is often advisable to take malaria precautions when visiting such areas, although the disease itself is still uncommon in most of the region. Leishmaniasis is also a potential concern (but is transmitted only by some sand flies, and these are active mainly at night and are most numerous in the dry season), so long sleeves and insect repellent are important to avoid insect bites. The flies should certainly not be a deterrent when it comes to planning a trip, since thousands of tourists visit these areas each year without getting sick.

> **SCARLET** and **GREEN-WINGED MACAWS** (*Ara macao* and *A. chloropterus*) gather at the Colorado clay lick close to the Tambopata Research Center in the lowlands of Amazonian Peru. Minerals in the clay help counteract toxins in the birds' mostly vegetarian diet.

CHESTNUT-CAPPED PUFFBIRD (*Bucco macrodactylus*) is an uncommon species that is found in both Várzea Forest (seasonally flooded) and Terra Firme Forest (dry year-round) at altitudes up to about 3,000 feet. It is patchily distributed through the Andean foothills of Colombia, Ecuador, and Peru and then across Amazonia to the east. It usually perches in the lower layers of the forest. Puffbirds are closest to jacamars in lineage and tend to sit still for long periods and remain fairly silent. They are sedentary, rarely moving far from their territories, and nest in burrows in rotted trunks or termite nests.

LITTLE CUCKOO (*Coccycua minuta*) resembles a smaller version of the familiar Squirrel Cuckoo but is mostly uniformly rufous except for the black-and-white tips to its tail feathers. It also lacks the gray belly of the Squirrel Cuckoo. The Little Cuckoo is a fairly uncommon and sought-after species by birders. Although widespread, it is generally confined to vegetation close to lakes and rivers. The species is found widely throughout Amazonia, reaching up to around 3,000 feet in the Andes, and is patchily distributed through Brazil to around São Paulo in the south.

GREATER ANI (*Crotophaga major*), unlike the dull black Groove- and Smooth-billedAnis, is a spectacular, large, glossy blue species with a larger bill and casque than its smaller cousins. It also has prominent paler edgings on the wing coverts and mantle, along with streaking on the breast. The piercing white iris of this species completes the picture of this dramatic, gothic-looking bird. Greater Anis are strongly associated with water and may be seen in flocks of up to twenty individuals foraging in thick vegetation. The species is found throughout northern South America south to northern Argentina and may be nomadic.

WHITE-THROATED JACAMAR (*Brachygalba albogularis*) is an unusual, small jacamar with an exceptionally long bill and prominent rictal bristles. It is associated with Várzea and riverine forest in the Amazonian lowlands at altitudes up to about 2,000 feet. It can sometimes be found alongside the larger Purus Jacamar—for example, in southeastern Peru around Puerto Maldanado. White-throated is more sociable than other jacamars and more likely to be found in small groups. It is patchily distributed in the lowlands of Peru and adjacent Amazonian Brazil.

MEALY PARROT (*Amazona farinosa*), **ORANGE-CHEEKED PARROT** (*Pyrilia barrabandi*), **BLUE-HEADED PARROT** (*Pionus menstruus*), and **DUSKY-HEADED PARAKEET** (*Aratinga weddellii*) are among the colorful parrots that attend the clay licks close to Tambopata Research Center, in southeastern Peru, where this picture was taken. Mealy Parrots are the common large Amazona parrots throughout much of the Andean lowlands and tend to be found in dense rain forest and forest edge along rivers. A pale grayish cast to the nape, visible on perched birds, is characteristic. Orange-cheeked Parrots are also widespread Amazonian birds that are often seen in tight flocks or, with luck, while foraging high in a fruiting tree. The other species pictured are depicted elsewhere in this book and are extremely distinctive when seen well.

BLUE-HEADED PARROT (*Pionus menstruus*) is a widespread, medium-sized parrot that can often be best recognized in flight by its deep wingbeats. It ranges from southern Central America through the Colombian Andes to the East Slope of Peru and across Amazonia to the Atlantic coast of Brazil. These attractive parrots are hard to see well and are most often encountered in flight. The photograph shows two young birds that have not yet developed the blue head of the adults. Their distinctively marked bills are a good identification feature, however; the upper mandible has a pink base.

RED-BREASTED MEADOWLARK (*Leistes militaris*) is the northern counterpart of the White-browed Meadowlark of central and southern South America. Striking male Red-breasteds usually sing from a slightly elevated perch surrounded by open, grassy fields or pastures. This is another species that is benefiting from Amazonian forest clearance—for example, around the town of Puerto Maldanado, in southeastern Peru, where this photo was taken.

WATTLED JACANA (*Jacana jacana*) is an active and intriguing resident of wetlands and marshy areas across the Amazon and throughout most of South America north of the Southern Cone. Two forms are in the Andean region: the black-backed population is found in western Colombia and ranges north into Central America, while the chestnut-backed form (pictured) is found elsewhere in the region, including across Amazonia. The bright yellow flight feathers—which can be seen as the birds fly or forage actively—are unmistakable. Jacanas are known for their exceptionally long toes, which help them walk across marsh vegetation without sinking.

RUFOUS MOTMOT

(*Baryphthengus martii*) is similar to the sympatric Broad-billed Motmot in general appearance but is much larger, lacks the green chin, and has less extensive green on the underparts. The Rufous Motmot ranges from Central America to Bolivia and east into Amazonia. Like other motmots, it tends to remain motionless for long periods except for the side-to-side motion of its tail (which may be a response to a perceived predator, such as a human). It feeds primarily on insects, but may include amphibians and lizards, as well as fruit, in its diet. It nests in a deep burrow in an earthen bank, like other motmots.

TURKEY VULTURE

(*Cathartes aura*) is one of the most widespread birds in the Americas, ranging from Canada to Argentina—with extralimital records from as far north as the North Slope of Alaska and regular occurrences as far south as the southern tip of Tierra del Fuego. These spectacular birds are among the greatest fliers of the bird world, able to turn seemingly effortlessly with almost no movement of their wings. They scavenge for dead animals using scent as their guide. They have longer wings than Black Vultures and hold them above their head and body in a dihedral when they soar and glide. Amazonian and East Slope birds (pictured) have a distinctive condor-like white nuchal collar.

PALM TANAGER (*Thraupis palmarum*) is found throughout the lowlands of northern South America in a variety of habitats often associated with palms, but not exclusively so. It is often one of the first species of tanager seen on an Amazonian birding trip, as it is frequently found in the gardens of large hotels and in urban areas with trees. The species tends to look gray and drab from a distance or in poor light—but like many apparently nondescript birds, it has a subtle beauty when seen close-up.

PURUS JACAMAR (*Galbalcyrhynchus purusianus*) replaces the slightly more widespread White-eared Jacamar in the central and southeastern Amazon of Peru. Purus has a relatively limited distribution on the East Slope of Peru, then reaching into Brazil's western Amazon and extending south into northern Bolivia. Its plumage is mostly a warm brown to wine-red color, contrasted with a large pink bill and eye ring and dark wings and tail. It has an association with water, including oxbow lakes. These unusual birds tend to sit still for long periods before expertly sallying to capture flying insects.

MASKED CRIMSON TANAGER (*Ramphocelus nigrogularis*) is another species found primarily in Amazonia that also ranges slightly into the Andean foothills at altitudes up to about 3,000 feet. The male's smart plumage is really striking; it's certain to make birders say "wow" at first sight. Several of the *Ramphocelus* tanagers (e.g., Black-bellied and Silver-beaked) are variations on a theme, with differing amounts of red and black in their plumage and a large, pale lower mandible, but the Masked Crimson Tanager might be the most dramatically colored of them all. It is commonly found near rivers and ranges through the lower eastern slopes of the Andes from Colombia to Peru, barely spilling over into Bolivia in the south, and it also occurs in the western and central Brazilian Amazon.

BANANAQUIT (*Coereba flaveola*) is one of the most familiar neotropical birds and ranges from Mexico and the Caribbean to Brazil and across much of tropical South America. The birds found in the Andes have pale gray throats and morphology varies across the species' range (those found in parts of the Caribbean have dark throats, for example). These active and unique birds are often found drinking from hummingbird feeders, where they use their sharp, decurved bills to access the sugar solution.

AMAZONIAN PARROTLET

(*Nannopsittaca dachilleae*) is an uncommon species with a fairly limited range in Peru, Bolivia, and adjoining Amazonian Brazil, and it has a strong association with bamboo. It is not especially well marked, but its blue crown distinguishes it from other small parrotlets in the region. Males of the two confusion species—Cobalt-rumped and Dusky-billed Parrotlets (both of which are members of the genus *Forpus*, rather than *Nannopsittaca*)— also have blue in their wings, which is lacking in this species. These small, cute parrots can be seen attending clay licks, like these birds, which were photographed at Tambopata Research Center, in southeastern Peru.

ORINOCO GOOSE (*Oressochen jubatus*) has a patchy distribution throughout the Amazonian region of northern and central South America. Birds are most often seen on the banks of large rivers, such as the Tambopata, where they form pairs or small family groups and tend to walk away from boats, rather than flying. Technically, this species is more closely related to the shelducks (*Tadorna*) than to true geese, and some populations are migratory. It appears to have declined in parts of its range (including in Peru), likely due to hunting, and is classified as Near Threatened by BirdLife.

DUSKY-HEADED PARAKEET (*Aratinga weddellii*) is a distinctive, medium-sized parakeet of the lowlands, reaching altitudes up to about 2,000 feet in the foothills. These attractive and unusual parakeets are strongly tied to rivers and to Várzea Forest, frequently using riverine clay licks in the Tambopata area of Peru, for example. They are often encountered in flocks that have a distinctive flight pattern: they regularly twist from side to side, allowing their blue wing coverts and secondaries to become visible. They have an association with bamboo and may gather in flocks to feed in thickets of seeding bamboo at times. The species ranges from the East Slope of the Andes into Amazonia and occurs from Colombia to Bolivia.

WHITE-FACED WHISTLING-DUCK (*Dendrocygna viduata*) is a distinctive, long-necked duck with a namesake white face, black-and-chestnut neck, and barred underparts. Like the Fulvous Whistling-Duck, it also ranges outside the Americas—in this case, also occurring across western and eastern Africa. These birds feed actively at night and can form very large flocks in habitats such as rice paddies and marshes.

YELLOWISH PIPIT (*Anthus chii*) is the only pipit likely to be encountered across most of the lowlands from Panama to Argentina. This is a nondescript species—some might say a typical pipit—but it really distinguishes itself when it comes to its buzzy and ticking song, which may be given in flight. Yellowish Pipits are found in flat, open areas with grass or in marshy habitats. This bird, for example, was photographed close to a series of rice paddies outside of the town of Puerto Maldonado in Peru.

COCOI HERON (*Ardea cocoi*) is the common large heron of Amazonia and the equivalent of North America's Great Blue Heron or Eurasia's Gray Heron (though note that the Great Blue overlaps with the Cocoi in parts of northern South America). The Cocoi Heron's main distinguishing characteristic, apart from its large size, is its striking black cap and contrasting white neck. These herons are found throughout the South American continent.

SCARLET, RED-AND-GREEN, and **BLUE-AND-YELLOW MACAWS** (*Ara macao*, *A. chloropterus*, and *A. ararauna*, respectively) are among the most spectacular birds of the neotropics. Widespread in lowland forest, these species are strongly associated with Amazonia, although Scarlet and Blue-and-yellow Macaws also extend into Central America. In the Tambopata region of Peru, these macaws (along with many other parrot species) gather in large groups at clay licks, where they ingest clay and minerals that help to counteract the toxins present in some of their food plants.

GOULD'S JEWELFRONT (*Heliodoxa aurescens*) is a stunning, relatively large, but uncommon lowland hummingbird that reaches altitudes up to about 4,500 feet along the eastern slope of the Andes. It is patchily distributed from southern Colombia to Bolivia and is also found in parts of Amazonia to the east. The stunning male, with its orange breast and violet crown, is a dazzling sight in the humid undergrowth of the Amazonian rain forest.

RUDDY GROUND DOVE (*Columbina talpacoti*) is a familiar, small ground dove that ranges from the southern United States to northern Argentina. It is found widely throughout the Andes and Amazonia and is a common bird of towns and agricultural areas. These ground doves frequently perch on overhead wires (where their diminutive size becomes obvious), and forage on the ground. The rufous males and grayer females often seem to wait until the last possible second before flying up from a road or roadside to avoid an oncoming vehicle.

SOUTHERN LAPWING (*Vanellus chilensis*) is a widespread and highly visible (and audible) large plover found in wet areas and open grasslands across a broad range in Central and South America. These distinctive birds use small pink spurs at their carpal joints both in display and, reportedly, to fend off predators. Southern Lapwings are replaced by the smaller Andean Lapwing in the highlands above about 9,500 feet.

CAPPED HERON (*Pilherodius pileatus*) is truly one of the most stately and gorgeous South American waterbirds. It is found in a variety of wetland settings, especially along large rivers, including the Tambopata of Peru, which flows into Amazonia from the Andean foothills. The full range extends from Panama to east-central South America, and the species has a strong association with Amazonia.

RAZOR-BILLED CURASSOW (*Mitu tuberosum*) is a large, spectacular curassow of the Amazonian lowlands, where it ranges from eastern Peru to northern Bolivia and into the Brazilian Amazon. These birds can occasionally be seen walking on the forest floor, but they also spend a lot of time in trees—sometimes high up—and it is easy to walk right below them without knowing they are there. Familiarity with the species' booming call is likely to help locate them, but be ready for a decent dose of "curassow neck" after you scan the limbs and canopy above your head.

THE SOUTHEASTERN DRY FOOTHILLS

GRAYISH BAYWING (*Agelaioides badius*) is widely distributed in southeastern South America, reaching into the tropical Andes in Bolivia. It is often seen in large flocks feeding around farms and in open habitats with few trees. These smart "blackbirds" are one of the least typical members of the family Icteridae based on plumage. Most other members have a combination of black and bright colors, but this species is entirely grayish brown with rufous flight feathers. Like nests made by the Chopi Blackbird, baywing nests are often parasitized by Shiny Cowbirds.

THE SOUTHEASTERN DRY FOOTHILLS > BIOGEOGRAPHY AND HISTORY

While the Andes Mountains continue south almost to the tip of South America, the Tropic of Capricorn, which currently lies just over twenty-three degrees south of the equator, is the limit of the geographic remit of this book. The area of the Andes that lies in the most southeasterly portion of this tropical region is the southeastern dry foothills of Bolivia. This area is sometimes referred to as the dry inter-Andean valleys and extends from the Cochabamba to Santa Cruz Departments, also touching Chuquisaca and Potosí. The area is comprised primarily of Central Andean Thornscrub. Similar habitats occur elsewhere in the Andes—around Quito, Ecuador, for example. These dry habitats tend to result from the rain-shadow effect caused by surrounding Andean peaks.

The foothills lie in the rain shadow of the Bolivian highlands, yet unlike areas of the East Slope to the immediate north, these dry mountains and valleys are not cloaked in humid cloud forest or typical yungas forest, but a mixture of xeric scrub and thorn forest known as Dry Deciduous Yungas that is more reminiscent of the Tumbesian and Marañón regions far to the north, in northwestern Peru and southwestern Ecuador. Somewhat similar habitats are found in parts of northern Bolivia, too, where species such as the Palkachupa Cotinga and Inti Tanager can be found. The dry climate of the southeastern foothills is punctuated by occasional summer storms that can dump significant rainfall in short periods. At the time of writing, the area is undergoing a period of significant drought that appears to be related to glacial reduction in the highlands—driven by climate change—with traditional watercourses, such as the Mizque River, all but dried up in November of 2023, for example. Note that glacial reduction in the Andes is significant and among the most pronounced on Earth. To their east, these foothills give way to Chaco woodlands and grasslands, to Espinal (an arid, thorny forest type), and to drier riparian evergreen forests, rather than the humid lowland rain forests of Amazonia that also lie to the north. Typical plants of the southeastern dry foothills include *Koeberlinia* (crown of thorns), columnar cacti such as *Lophocereus* and *Opuntia* (prickly pear), *Agave*, and *Parkinsonia* (paloverde), with its thorns and characteristic light green bark. The general impression of the region is of a semi-desert-like environment surrounded by the reds and browns of the mountain slopes and cliffs that are typical of this area. It holds a stark beauty and also has a unique biological character that connects it both to the Andes and to the dry savannas and forests of the Bolivian lowlands.

This region is rich in history and has been subject to the control of several different cultures since about 1000 CE—first by the Tiahuanaco Empire, which centered itself close to the southeastern edge of Lake Titicaca about 600 BCE, then, after its collapse in about 1200 CE, by the seven regional kingdoms of the Aymara people that became dominant in the region—including over the Uru, another important ethnic group in the area. The Aymara themselves were eventually conquered by the Incas in the fifteenth century, although the Aymara society remained fairly intact under Inca rule. Of course, the Incas were also then conquered by the Spanish, and, finally, modern-day Bolivia was founded on August 6, 1825, when it declared independence from Spain. Interestingly, the Inca language (Quechua) is still spoken in this area, and local clothing has much in common with the Peruvian highlands, demonstrating the widespread influence of the Incas.

GUIRA CUCKOO (*Guira guira*) is widespread across much of eastern and southern South America in dry, open habitats and around settlements and farm fields. When seen close-up, this species looks more like a creature from a Harry Potter movie than a real bird, especially its head, which resembles that of a griffin or hippogriff. Guira Cuckoos are often encountered in noisy groups but, like most cuckoos, can easily melt into any small tree or bush they land in, despite their size and ungainly appearance.

THE SOUTHEASTERN DRY FOOTHILLS > BIRD DIVERSITY AND SPECIALTIES

This area has relatively lower overall bird diversity than humid areas to the north, but it does harbor characteristic species that make it a special and important area for birds and birding. While hummingbird diversity is much lower than in areas of cloud forest and other humid habitats, parrot diversity and abundance is especially high here. Rufous Horneros, with their domed mud nests, are quite common and are among the prominent species connecting this area to habitats in the eastern lowlands. Likewise, the Creamy-bellied Thrush, a partial austral migrant, can be common here, as it is throughout the eastern lowlands of Bolivia. Conversely, the area also harbors species that are more characteristic of the high Andes, such as the Andean Condor. Relatively few neotropical passerine migrants are found this far south, but species such as the Swainson's Thrush and Western Wood-Pewee have been recorded.

The real star of the show in relation to this habitat is the spectacular and Critically Endangered Red-fronted Macaw, which is found nowhere else. These showy macaws nest semicolonially on cliffs in the canyons of the region and are a flagship species for conservation here. Other parrots, too, make a home on these cliffs, including noisy Mitred Parakeets; Cliff Parakeets (split by some authorities from the similar and more widespread Monk Parakeet), with their giant stick nests; and colorful Turquoise-fronted Parrots. Tight flocks of Yellow-chevroned Parakeets can often be seen, too, skimming the tops of the columnar cacti as they hurtle past, as can the distinctive red-tailed and intricately marked Green-cheeked Parakeets. Hummingbirds include the spectacular Blue-tufted Starthroat, the widespread Glittering-bellied Emerald, and the White-bellied Hummingbird.

Other common species that in combination are characteristic of the area include the White-fronted Woodpecker, Bolivian Blackbird, Picui Ground Dove, White-tipped Dove, Guira Cuckoo, Scissor-tailed Nightjar, Andean Swift, Cliff Flycatcher, Spot-backed Puffbird, Narrow-billed Woodcreeper, White-tipped Plantcutter, Ringed Warbling-Finch, Greater Wagtail-Tyrant, and the ubiquitous Rufous-collared Sparrow and Sayaca Tanager.

CONSERVATION — THE SOUTHEASTERN DRY FOOTHILLS

Only two globally threatened birds are found in this area: the Vulnerable Andean Condor and the Critically Endangered and endemic Red-fronted Macaw. Additionally, two more Bolivian endemics, Ringed Warbling-Finch and Bolivian Blackbird, can also be seen here (as can a fourth if you include Cliff Parakeet, which some authorities split from Monk Parakeet). The primary bird conservation concern is for the macaw, which always seems to have had a limited global distribution but has likely been further reduced in population due to poaching and persecution as a crop pest. The species has an estimated population of just six hundred to eight hundred individuals in four subpopulations. One of the greatest concentrations is found at the Red-fronted Macaw Reserve, established and managed with local communities by Asociación Armonía with support from American Bird Conservancy. This single site has approximately forty breeding pairs of the macaw, which nest on the reserve's tall cliffs. Armonía has formed a partnership with local people and is developing bird tourism in the area, with proceeds shared with the community. Reserve staff began placing peanuts in a small field at the base of the cliff in 2019 as a means of attracting macaws back to the area after disturbance from road construction. This has continued since, and it may also encourage the macaws to avoid raiding local crops, since they now have an alternative food supply. The organization has also installed nest boxes on the cliffs to increase the number of potentially available nesting sites.

There are additional community-run protected areas within the southeastern dry foothills region, such as at Pasorapa and Lagarpampa, and conservation capacity is building to ensure that conservation management of these sites can be expanded. Visitors staying at the macaw reserve itself pay $200 per night, which may seem expensive for a basic lodge in rural Bolivia, but the cost of staying here covers much more than the room and board. Funds are divided among community members, helping the project become sustainable in the long term and supporting activities such as community education and the reserve's own management costs. In the past, poaching was a major problem, and community members were focused more on protecting their crops from parrots than on protecting parrots from poachers. This changed with the advent of the reserve and lodge—which means that the wild macaws are now more valuable to the community—and poaching by outsiders for the bird markets in Santa Cruz and elsewhere has been more or less eliminated. As a whole, the habitat in this area is not highly threatened, and apart from some river valleys, it is mostly too arid for farming and grazing. So long as the threat of poaching can be contained, there is a strong chance that the Red-fronted Macaw can eventually be downgraded from Critically Endangered to Endangered.

WHITE-TIPPED PLANTCUTTER (*Phytotoma rutila*) is one of three species of plantcutter that are part of the cotinga family, and all are confined to South America. These unique birds feed largely on leaves and other plant materials and have a serrated bill that helps to cut the foliage. This species is found in central southern South America in a variety of habitats, including urban areas (such as around the city of Cochabamba, Bolivia), as well as in dry forest. Plantcutters can often be best detected by their weird, buzzy, complaining calls. Males and females differ in appearance: the male has warm rufous underparts combined with gray upperparts, and the female is brown and streaky overall.

BIRDING AND PHOTOGRAPHY SITES | THE SOUTHEASTERN DRY FOOTHILLS

Probably the top birding and photography site in this area is the Red-fronted Macaw Reserve near Perereta, operated by local Quechua community members in association with Asociación Armonía. In order to stay here, it is essential to book well in advance through reservations@armonia-bo.org. Arranging transport is also important, as there are relatively few ways to get to this remote site, despite it lying within about a half-mile of a major highway. The reserve has a nice lodge and good food and is an excellent base from which to explore the surrounding area. The garden in front of the lodge has feeders and attracts most of the key species that a visitor would want to see and photograph, such as White-fronted Woodpecker and Bolivian Blackbird.

Wandering through the dry forest along the Mizque River allows visitors to find additional species not present in the lodge garden. When the river is in flood, access is more challenging but still possible. It is best to consult Armonía in advance about access relative to water levels. The best time to visit to see Red-fronted Macaws is between November and early May. Each morning, the reserve warden provides supplemental peanuts to the birds, in part to dissuade them from raiding agricultural crops nearby. A small blind is directly adjacent to the feeding area, and this is a great place to photograph these spectacular parrots. The macaws can also be seen and photographed from the clifftop close to the main road, about fifteen minutes by car from the lodge. In the morning, it is not uncommon to see Andean Condors soaring overhead, and other raptors, such as Black-chested Buzzard-Eagles, can sometimes fly close to the cliff, causing consternation among the macaws and other parrots. The road to the lodge often has Scissor-tailed Nightjars that can be found at night by looking for their eye shine while using a good flashlight or your car headlamps. Small birds will respond to imitations of the song of the Ferruginous Pygmy-Owl; when used sparingly, this can sometimes be a good way (in addition to waiting at the feeders) to find tody-flycatchers, wagtail-tyrants, and other species in the riparian woodland. Many of the smaller parrots are most frequently seen only in fast-flying groups, although the macaws are reliably photographed at close range from the blind. The same cannot generally be said for Yellow-chevroned and Green-cheeked Parakeets, which are less predictable and flightier. Note that Blue-tufted Starthroat does not seem to come to the hummingbird feeders in the lodge yard and is more likely to be found patrolling territories around flowering groups of prickly pear cacti.

WHITE-FRONTED WOODPECKER (*Melanerpes cactorum*) is an appealing, animated, small woodpecker with a limited range in the central part of southern South America. It is strongly associated with Chaco (lowland dry broadleaf forest) and other semiarid habitats, and especially areas with columnar cacti. White-fronted Woodpeckers have a habit of raising their wings in a territorial display while perched high on cacti, which can make for an excellent photograph. Like many other woodpeckers, the male is distinguished by its red rear crown, which is black in the female.

MITRED PARAKEET (*Psittacara mitratus*) is a member of a group of similar species that require care to separate. Knowing the species' calls can help, but most birders will also want to see the specific plumage differences to be satisfied with their identifications. All the species—Mitred, White-eyed, Red-masked, and Scarlet-fronted Parakeets—exhibit slight differences in facial and wing patterns, and the location and amount of the red feathering on their face and body is key to unlocking their identities. Mitred is most similar to Red-masked, based on the extent of red on its face, but Mitred lacks the red shoulder patch of that species. Mitred Parakeets are found from Ecuador to northern Argentina, primarily along the humid East Slope, at altitudes from about 5,000 to 11,000 feet.

SHINY COWBIRD (*Molothrus bonariensis*) is a small, sharp-billed, glossy icterid that is one of the most widespread neotropical birds (female pictured). In South America, it is absent from the heart of Amazonia, the altiplano, and Tierra del Fuego but is commonly found in the right habitat in most other parts of the continent, as well as through the Caribbean and, occasionally, in the southern United States. These birds are nest parasites, like other cowbirds, and are well named, since the males have a strong glossy sheen and the species is often associated with cattle.

CREAMY-BELLIED THRUSH (*Turdus amaurochalinus*) is widespread in central and southern South America and is at least a partial austral migrant. It is found in open, often dry habitats, including thorn forest, as well as in urban parks and developed areas. This species is superficially similar to several other mostly brown South American thrushes, and care should be taken if identification is based on brief views, especially if the head is not seen well. The dark lores and yellow (or brown and yellow) bill of this species can be helpful in clinching an identification.

RED-FRONTED MACAW (*Ara rubrogenys*) is found only in the dry southeastern foothills of the Bolivian Andes. Considered Critically Endangered, and with a global population of no more than eight hundred individuals, it is easy to see why this spectacular species is sought after by the wild bird trade. Recent conservation measures led by Asociación Armonía are ensuring that key populations are well protected from poaching, however. Armonía has established the Red-fronted Macaw Reserve, which is managed by local community members, so visitors can see this gorgeous species in the wild. COUNTRY ENDEMIC (BOLIVIA). CR

TURQUOISE-FRONTED PARROT (*Amazona aestiva*) is found across the central part of South America, preferring drier, more open woodlands south of Amazonia. It also occurs on the dry eastern slopes of the Bolivian Andes. This species is vividly colored, and this shows best in flight, when its red inner primaries become more visible. Like other Amazona parrots, Turquoise-fronted Parrots have rapid, shallow wingbeats and, with practice, can be recognized by call. They nest on the cliffs at Armonía's Red-fronted Macaw Reserve, which is a good place to see them, along with several other parrot species.

The **MASKED GNATCATCHER** (*Polioptila dumicola*) is a smartly plumaged resident of the dry Andean foothills of Bolivia, as well as of open savanna woodlands to the south and east. In the Andes, at altitudes above about 2,500 feet, you can find the darker *saturata* subspecies (pictured), in which the underparts are much duskier gray than in lowland populations.

GRAY-CRESTED FINCH (*Lophospingus griseocristatus*) is another species lost from the finches and added to the tangers due to DNA analysis. These distinctive birds are found from Bolivia to northern Argentina and can be seen in open thorn scrub, as well as in other dry habitats where they may be expanding due to deforestation. A good place to see them is at Armonía's Red-fronted Macaw Reserve, which lies a few hours' drive southeast of Cochabamba, Bolivia.

MONK PARAKEET (*Myiopsitta monachus*) is a familiar bird to many, as it is commonly kept as a pet and escaped birds have established themselves in the United States. In central Bolivia, a population of this species (known as the Cliff Parakeet)—which is split as a separate species by some authorities—builds its giant stick nests on cliffs (often alongside other parrots, including the Red-fronted Macaw). These central Bolivian birds, of the *luchsi* subspecies (pictured), also have a whiter face and breast than most Monk Parakeets, and more yellow on the underparts.

CHOPI BLACKBIRD (*Gnorimopsar chopi*) is named for one of its most frequent calls, a double-noted *cho-pee*. This species is widespread from the southeastern Amazon region east to the Brazilian Atlantic coast, and it ranges into the tropical Andes in Bolivia, where it is widespread in the western Amazon and foothills. These gregarious icterids lack the gloss of Shiny Cowbirds (which sometimes parasitize their nests) and are chunkier overall. They seem to be benefiting from deforestation in some areas, since they are adapted to open habitats, but the potential for escaped cagebirds (they are frequently kept as pets) may mask distributional changes.

YELLOW-CHEVRONED PARAKEET (*Brotogeris chiriri*) is a small, mainly green parakeet that is widespread across the drier woodlands and savannas south of Amazonia and also occurs in lowland forest along rivers. It also reaches into the tropical Andean foothills in eastern Bolivia. These birds are shy and tend to roam in small, fast-flying groups that seem to be in constant motion. The species was formerly considered conspecific with the White-winged Parakeet, which has a more northerly East Slope and Amazonian distribution, but is now treated as separate species.

PICUI GROUND DOVE (*Columbina picui*) is widespread in open habitats throughout southeastern South America, reaching into the tropical Andes in Bolivia. These attractive, delicate, small doves are often found in pairs foraging on the ground. They always appear extremely pale but in flight also show a black-and-white wing pattern. The thin line of blue feathers on the wing coverts is hard to see except when the birds are close-up, but they can be confiding, if given time to approach you as they search for food.

SAYACA TANAGER (*Thraupis sayaca*) essentially replaces the Blue-gray Tanager in southeastern South America. East of the Andes, Blue-gray Tanagers have white shoulders and wing bars, so adult Sayaca Tanagers (which lack these features) are normally readily identified (the two species may overlap in parts of the Bolivian Andes south to Cochabamba). However, young birds can be almost impossible to separate in the field. These attractive and fairly common tanagers favor open country and can be found in urban areas as well as in parks and agricultural lands.

> **FROM THE FIELD** — Personal stories from the leaders of American Bird Conservancy's primary bird and habitat conservation partners in the tropical Andes.

CHAMPIONING COMMUNITY CONSERVATION FOR ENDEMIC MACAWS AND BIRD DIVERSITY IN BOLIVIA

IN 1996, BOLIVIA had a population of just 7.15 million people, making it the least densely populated country in South America, with only seven individuals per square kilometer. During that year, at the age of sixteen, I began venturing out on my own to explore the vast, sparsely populated areas where nature thrived in my country. I was completely mesmerized by the lush and arid forests I encountered; the diversity of animals and plants was simply enchanting. This pivotal moment in my life led me to pursue a degree in biology at the Universidad Mayor de San Simón.

During my university years, I crossed paths with a German student, Sebastian Herzog, who was conducting his doctoral research on birds. Through a mutual friend, José Balderrama, I was invited to join Sebastian in his fieldwork. This introduction to the world of birdwatching sparked an obsession with ornithology. While I knew that Bolivia's species richness was astounding, getting up close and personal with the birds was truly out of this world.

After completing my studies, Sebastian and Bennett Hennessey extended me an invitation to join their organization, Armonía, in March 2003. Together, they were reshaping Armonía to become Bolivia's pioneer organization dedicated to preventing bird extinctions. This alignment of my passions propelled me to join the team without a second thought.

At that time, the conservation and birdwatching cultures in Bolivia were in their infancy. Our efforts were concentrated on education and research, aiming to raise awareness about birds and to identify key conservation sites to prevent bird extinctions.

Transitioning from being an explorer, I focused on implementing strategies to safeguard the Horned Curassow from extinction in the protected areas of Amboró, Carrasco, and the Isiboro Sécure National Park and Indigenous Territory. These regions faced encroachment by Andean families seeking new opportunities, leading to coca cultivation. It became evident that these protected areas alone would not suffice; equally important was integrating sustainable development strategies to protect the curassow and its habitat.

In September 2005, I relocated to Germany to pursue a PhD in biodiversity and ecology at the University of Göttingen. There I delved into analyzing diversity and endemism patterns and their correlation with climatic, topographic, and anthropogenic factors. The diverse community I encountered broadened my understanding across scientific, socioeconomic, and philosophical realms, enriching my conservation knowledge.

Upon my return to Bolivia in 2011, I rejoined Armonía, witnessing the organization's remarkable achievements despite challenges from the country's political landscape. Armonía's partnerships with American Bird Conservancy, BirdLife International, World Land Trust, and others provided a robust foundation for its conservation initiatives.

Assuming the role of Armonía's first Bolivian executive director in 2017, I leveraged enhanced tools and knowledge to further integrate conservation efforts with sustainable development for local communities, striving for the financial sustainability of on-the-ground conservation programs involving local stakeholders.

After twenty-seven years, I proudly affirm that Armonía, as a collective, has successfully reversed the declining population trend of Bolivia's endemic macaw species, restored critical high Andean habitats for numerous threatened and endemic bird species in Bolivia's *Polylepis* forests, nurtured a burgeoning culture of birdwatching and nature conservation, and initiated diverse conservation actions to protect other endangered bird species. These accomplishments were made possible through the unwavering support of, and collaboration with, our international partners, notably American Bird Conservancy.

DR. RODRIGO W. SORIA AUZA
Executive Director, Asociación Armonía

RED-FRONTED MACAW (*Ara rubrogenys*) is among the most endangered of the macaws and is restricted to a small area in the southeastern Andes of Bolivia. These appealing, colorful birds can be photographed from a blind at Armonía's reserve along the Mizque River where one of the largest populations of the species nests on the spectacular cliffs overlooking the lodge. This remote site is also a great place to see and photograph many of the other specialty birds of the region.

MIGRATION TO AND FROM THE TROPICAL ANDES

HERE ARE JUST a few of the many species that migrate from North America to the tropical Andes every year. These delicate creatures, some weighing as little as a penny, then fly as many as 4,000 miles back from South America to get to their spring and summer habitats each year. You may be able to see some of these species in your own backyard, or at one of their favorite resting spots nearby. If you scan the QR code on this page, you will be able to click on any of the photos in a web gallery and learn, among other interesting things, their conservation status, as well as hear their songs and calls. These photos were all taken in the United States.

YELLOW-BILLED CUCKOO
(*Coccyzus americanus*)

BLACK-BILLED CUCKOO
(*Coccyzus erythropthalmus*)

SOLITARY SANDPIPER
(*Tringa solitaria*)

LESSER YELLOWLEGS
(*Tringa flavipes*)

GREAT-CRESTED FLYCATCHER
(*Myiarchus crinitus*)

EASTERN KINGBIRD
(*Tyrannus tyrannus*)

EASTERN WOOD-PEWEE
(*Contopus virens*)

WILLOW FLYCATCHER
(*Empidonax traillii*)

RED-EYED VIREO
(*Vireo olivaceus*)

BARN SWALLOW
(*Hirundo rustica*)

GRAY-CHEEKED THRUSH
(*Catharus minimus*)

SWAINSON'S THRUSH
(*Catharus ustulatus*)

BALTIMORE ORIOLE
(*Icterus galbula*)

NORTHERN WATERTHRUSH
(*Parkesia noveboracensis*)

BLACK-AND-WHITE WARBLER
(*Mniotilta varia*)

TENNESSSEE WARBLER
(*Leiothlypis peregrina*) immature

CONNECTICUT WARBLER
(*Oporornis agilis*)

PROTHONOTARY WARBLER
(*Protonotaria citrea*)

PROTHONOTARY WARBLER
(*Protonotaria citrea*)

AMERICAN REDSTART
(*Setophaga ruticilla*) male

AMERICAN REDSTART
(*Setophaga ruticilla*) female

BAY-BREASTED WARBLER
(*Setophaga castanea*)

BLACKBURNIAN WARBLER
(*Setophaga fusca*)

BLACKPOLL WARBLER
(*Setophaga striata*) immature

SCARLET TANAGER
(*Piranga olivacea*)

SCARLET TANAGER (*Piranga olivacea*)
transitional plumage

ROSE-BREASTED GROSBEAK
(*Pheucticus ludovicianus*)

CANADA WARBLER
(*Cardellina canadensis*)

SUMMER TANAGER
(*Piranga rubra*) sub-adult male

ROSE-BREASTED GROSBEAK
(*Pheucticus ludovicianus*)

PHOTOGRAPHER'S STATEMENT

WHILE THE BEAUTY of nature has always enchanted me, birds, more than any of the other creatures or wonders, have totally captured my imagination. During the last two decades, I have traveled around the world to find and photograph these exquisitely beautiful and elusive creatures. I have found the range of color and design of the avian populations to be mind-boggling, and I love the challenges of capturing their beauty with my camera.

My commercial work was largely fashion. Photographing birds is as far to the extreme opposite of fashion photography as one can get. I can sum up the difference in one word—control. Whether shooting in the studio or on location as a fashion photographer, I could organize the set, direct the models, and control the lighting, backgrounds, and environment. Not so easy, shooting birds! I travel for hours to get to the habitats, and we begin our days before dawn. What keeps me going after hours on my feet, often in hot and buggy environments, when I am exhausted, as I was most days as we traveled in the upper elevations of the high Andes, is the feeling of excitement and expectation. I keep pushing myself because I know that I am going to get the photos I am looking for. If I get tired, I look at the images I have already made that day, and I get pumped up. My heart begins to pound, and I once again feel how lucky I am to be doing this work. I find happiness in searching out these exquisite creatures, some so vulnerable; capturing their images to share with you is the thrill of a lifetime and continues to give meaning to my life. To do something I am passionate about for as long as I am able is a gift I am grateful for every day. When I feel I have accomplished what I hope to, it thrills me. My hope is to share that emotional intensity with the people who see my photographs. I want people to feel the same excitement I do when I see on the back of my camera the image of a bird that made my heart soar.

I have been a Nikon shooter for more than fifty years. I know that other camera systems are probably equally as good, but I'm still happy that I have stuck with Nikon. The new mirrorless cameras are thrilling to use, but in some ways, they and the new lenses present a double-edged sword for me, since I am forced with each advancement to spend what seems like endless time mastering the new equipment. I have come to realize that I must push myself more than ever to keep up. I could easily use cameras I mastered years ago, but among other advancements of this new technology is the keeper rate, the percentage of pictures that are sharp and exposed correctly. There has never been anything like it.

What makes a great photo? I realize that this question is totally subjective; everybody will have a different opinion. For me, a great picture is one that moves me emotionally, that makes my heart soar. It's a goal I can't always accomplish, but it keeps me going, keeps me working harder. The important elements are the center of focus, depth of field, background, and foreground. What does the photo tell us about the environment? Does the composition work? Does it tell a story? Although it's capturing the beauty of the birds that brings me there, it's the sum of all these elements that completes the photo for me. A case in point is the cover photo of this book.

I am an artist who uses as many of the state-of-the-art digital tools as I can to create a work of art that will get more people to care about birds, the environment, and conservation. The images, character, and behavior of the birds are not altered. We occasionally and sparingly use playback to attract species that would otherwise be virtually impossible to photograph well. Many birds are photographed in the vicinity of feeders that offer unparalleled opportunities to capture images of birds that otherwise skulk habitually or are found only high in the forest. No birds were photographed at the nest.

It has been a great privilege for me to return to photography, my first love, and it's my hope that readers of this book will be inspired by my passion for birds, my commitment to them, and my deep sense of the importance of the work of American Bird Conservancy.

ABOUT THE PHOTOGRAPHER

OWEN DEUTSCH, a Chicago native, had a twenty-year career as a fashion photographer. He retired in 1986 to devote his time to a second business, Loft Development Corporation, a company with a rich history as a pioneer in the practice of renovating old urban industrial warehouses and converting them into loft-style office spaces and other uses. In 2002, he was introduced to birding by a close friend who asked for help with his bird photography. A whole new world opened up to Owen, and he was hooked. He was back in the beauty business again, but this time, it was birds, butterflies, and all the magnificent creatures of nature in front of his lens. He travels all over the world in pursuit of his passion, and his extensive website is a way of sharing his love of birds with friends. *Chicago Tonight* on PBS station WTTW in Chicago aired a profile of him and his work, ranging from his fashion career to his bird photography. To see it, use the QR code below. Owen has an extensive following on social media. Follow along at @OwenDeutsch. This is his second book.

Scan the QR code to see WTTW feature on Owen

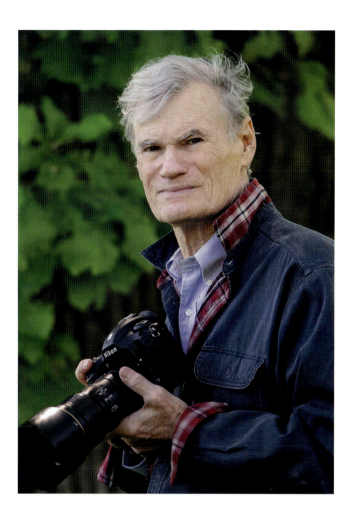

ABOUT THE AUTHOR

MICHAEL PARR has been a birder since he was seven years old, and he has worked in bird conservation since 1989. He joined American Bird Conservancy in 1996, after graduating from the University of East Anglia, United Kingdom, and working for BirdLife International. He became president of American Bird Conservancy in 2017. He has coauthored several books, including *Parrots: A Guide to Parrots of the World*, *The American Bird Conservancy Guide to the 500 Most Important Bird Areas in the United States*, and *The American Bird Conservancy Guide to Bird Conservation*, along with numerous articles and papers. He is also chair of the Alliance for Zero Extinction.

FURTHER READING

THE MAJORITY OF this book is based on personal field experience. Many of the bird-related facts were double-checked by using eBird and the BirdLife Data Zone. I also conducted additional online research and referred to several books about birds, ecology, and culture in the region; these works are mentioned below. In addition, I conducted interviews with bird and conservation experts, including indigenous people. At the time of writing, I have personally visited every major life zone and many of the locations mentioned in this book. Several other excellent online resources exist for birders and photographers who are planning to visit the Andes. These include the birdsong repository Xeno-Canto; Cloud Birders, which is a great resource for birding trip reports; BirdsEye, which enables you to download eBird data in an easy-to-use map-based format; and the itineraries of birding travel companies whose tours you may wish to join. Several of the books mentioned below also have associated smartphone apps that can be downloaded for use in the field; they can be extremely handy, since many of the books themselves are quite large. When planning a tour, it is often good to research local tourism operations as well as the better-known international companies. I hope you find these additional resources to be interesting and useful.

Campbell, I., et al. 2021. *Habitats of the World*. Princeton University Press.

Captivating History. 2022. *History of Latin America*.

del Hoyo, J., and Collar, N. J. 2014 and 2016. *Illustrated Checklist of the Birds of the World*. Vol. 1, *Non-Passerines*, and Vol. 2, *Passerines*. Lynx Edicions, Barcelona.

Faaborg, J. 2002. *Saving Migrant Birds*. University of Texas Press.

Fjeldså, J., and Krabbe, N. 1990. *Birds of the High Andes*. Zoological Museum of Copenhagen and Apollo Books.

Forsyth, A., and Miyata, K. 1984. *Tropical Nature*. Touchstone, New York.

Herzog, S., et al. 2016. *Birds of Bolivia*. Asociación Armonía, Santa Cruz de la Sierra, Bolivia.

Hilty, S. L., and Brown, W. L. 1986. *A Guide to the Birds of Colombia*. Princeton University Press.

Long A. J., et al. 1998. *Endemic Bird Areas of the World*. BirdLife International, Cambridge.

Medina, W., Huang, R. M., and Pimm, S. L. 2023. "Region-wide Retreats from Lower Elevations of Range-Restricted Birds across the Northern Andes." *Conservation Biology* 37, no. 5: e14127.

Ridgely, R. S., and Greenfield, P. J. 2001. *The Birds of Ecuador*. Helm Field Guides, London.

Rodrigues, P., and Micael, J. 2020. "The Importance of Guano Birds to the Inca Empire and the First Conservation Measures Implemented by Humans." *Ibis* 163, no. 1: 283–91.

Rosenberg, K. V., et al. 2019. "Decline of the North American Avifauna." *Science* 366, no. 6461: 120–24.

Schulenberg, T. S., et al. 2007. *Birds of Peru*. Princeton University Press.

Stotz, D. F., et al. 1996. *Neotropical Birds: Ecology and Conservation*. University of Chicago Press.

Terborgh, J. 1989. *Where Have All the Birds Gone?* Princeton University Press.

Wege, D. C., and Long, A. J. 1995. *Key Areas for Threatened Birds in the Neotropics*. BirdLife International, Cambridge.

Wellman, W. 2023. *The Inca Empire*. Enthralling History.

Wheatley, N. 1994. *Where to Watch Birds in South America*. Princeton Legacy Library.

INDEX

Page references in **bold** refer to photographs.

Adelomyia melanogenys 56
Agelaioides badius 240–241
Aglaeactis cupripennis 136
Aglaiocercus coelestis 45
Aglaiocercus kingii 205
Albatross, Chatham 73
  Waved 71, 73, 74
Amazona aestiva 250
Amazona farinosa 224–225
Amazona mercenarius 200
Amazonetta brasiliensis 214
Ampelion rubrocristatus 206
Anarhynchus alticola 176
Anas bahamensis 77
Anas flavirostris 170
Anas georgica 142
Andigena laminirostris 17
Ani, Greater 223
  Groove-billed 223
  Smooth-billed 223
Anisognathus notabilis 38
Anisognathus somptuosus 111
Antbird, Ash-breasted 216
  Bicolored 215
  Black-tailed 218
  Hairy-crested 215
  Ocellated 215
  White-cheeked 215
Anthus chii 233
Antpitta, Chestnut-crowned 25, 206
  Chestnut-naped 192
  Cundinamarca 97, 98, 182
  Equatorial 190
  Giant 14, 25, **26**
  Jocotoco 186, **187**, 189
  Moustached 25, **44**
  Ochre-breasted 25, **34**
  Ochre-fronted 186
  Pale-billed 178, 186
  Red-and-white 151
  Rufous 191
  Scaled 44
  Stripe-headed 148
  Tawny 137, 138, 141, 206
  Urubamba 151
  Yellow-breasted 25, **30**
Antshrike, Bar-crested 124
  Barred **124**
  Lined 124
  Uniform 53
Antthrush, Rufous-fronted 218
Ara ararauna 212–213, **235**

Ara chloropterus 212–213, 220–221, **234**
Ara macao 220–221, **234**
Ara rubrogenys **10–11**, 250, **257**
Aracari, Collared **43**, 49
Aratinga weddellii 224–225, **231**
Ardea cocoi **233**
Arremon aurantiirostris **210**
Arremon basilicus 110
Arremonops conirostris **123**
Arundinicola leucocephala 112
Asthenes dorbignyi **172**
Athene cunicularia **78–79**
Atlapetes fulviceps 152
Atlapetes latinuchus **195**
Atlapetes leucopterus **184**
Atlapetes melanocephalus **103**
Atlapetes tricolor 98
Aulacorhynchus albivitta **105**
Aulacorhynchus haemotopygus **39**
Avocet, Andean 13, **160**, 161, 165

Bananaquit **229**
Bangsia aureocincta **24**
Bangsia edwardsi **24**
Barbet, Red-headed 23
  Toucan 13, **25**
Bare-eye, Black-spotted **215**
Baryphthengus martii **226**
Baywing, Grayish 240–241
Becard, Barred **185**
  Slaty 54, **58**
Bittern, Least 74
  Pinnated 58
Blackbird, Bolivian **244**, 245, 247
  Chopi 240, **253**
Boissonneaua flavescens 9, **115**, 131
Boissonneaua jardini **37**
Boissonneaua matthewsii **202**
Booby, Blue-footed 88
  Peruvian 16, 71, 74, **88–89**
Brachygalba albogularis **223**
Brilliant, Empress **31**
  Fawn-breasted **201**
  Green-crowned 20, **21**, 183
  Violet-fronted **183**
Brotogeris chiriri **254**
Brushfinch, Antioquia 98
  Bay-crowned **185**
  Bolivian 152
  Fulvous-headed 152
  Pale-headed 48, 57, 58
  Pale-naped 98
  "Paynter's" 185
  Rufous-capped 98
  Santa Marta 103

Sierra Nevada 110
  Stripe-headed 110
  Tricolored **98**, 195
  White-winged **184**
  Yellow-breasted **195**
Bucco macrodactylus **222**
Bushbird, Recurve-billed 98
Bush Tanager, Black-backed 151
  Dusky **114**
  Dusky-bellied **114**
Buzzard-Eagle, Black-chested 13, 247

Cacique, Selva **218**
Calidris virgata **69**
Campephilus melanoleucos **191**
Campylopterus largipennis **197**
Canastero, Cactus 71, **72**, 73
  Creamy-breasted **172**
Caracara, Carunculated 138, **140**, 141
  Mountain 141, 148, 161, 165
Cardellina canadensis **259**
Catharus aura **227**
Catharus minimus **258**
Catharus ustulatus **199**, 258
Chachalaca, Colombian **109**
  Speckled 109
Chaetocercus mulsant **65**
Chalcothraupis ruficervix **126–127**
Chat-Tyrant, Brown-backed **147**
  Piura **61**
Chlorestes julie **46**
Chloroceryle amazona **104**
Chlorochrysa phoenicotis **31**
Chlorospingus, Dusky **114**
Chlorospingus semifuscus **114**
Chlorothraupis stolzmanni **36**
Chroicocephalus serranus **134–135**
Chrysuronia oenone **196**
Cinclodes, Bar-winged **169**
  Buff-winged 169
  Chestnut-winged 169
  Cream-winged **169**
  Royal 148, 149, 151
  Stout-billed 138, **143**
  Surf 71, 73, **91**
  White-bellied 75, 162, 165
Cinclodes albiventris **169**
Cinclodes excelsior **143**
Cinclodes taczanowskii **91**
Coccycua minuta **222**
Coccyzus americanus 258
Coccyzus erythropthalmus 258
Cock-of-the-rock, Andean 13, **95**, 185, 189

Coeligena lutetiae 97
Coeligena torquata 64, **180–181**
Coereba flaveola 229
Colaptes rupicola **175**
Colibri coruscans 62
Colibri cyanotus 202
Colibri delphinae **107**
Columbina picui **254**
Columbina squammata **127**
Columbina talpacoti **237**
Comet, Gray-bellied 57, **61**
  Red-tailed **148**, 161
Condor, Andean 13, 73, 75, 132, 138, 141, **148**, 244, 245, 247
Conebill, Giant **148**, **149**, 151
  Tamarugo 73
Conirostrum binghami **149**
Contopus fumigatus 30
Contopus virens 258
Coot, Giant 13, 161, **165**
  Slate-colored **74**, 165
Cormorant, Guanay 16, **66–67**, 74, 81
  Red-legged 74, **81**
Coronet, Buff-tailed 9, **115**, **131**
  Chestnut-breasted **186**, 202
  Velvet-purple 22, **37**
Cotinga, Palkachupa **242**
  Red-crested **148**, 151, **206**
  White-cheeked **149**
Cowbird, Shiny **240**, **248**, **253**
Crescentchest, Marañon 54, **61**
  Olive-crowned **148**
Crotophaga major **223**
Crypturellus soui **106**
Cuckoo, Black-billed 57, 258
  Guira **243**, 244
  Little **222**
  Squirrel **122**, **222**
  Yellow-billed 258
Curassow, Blue-billed **98**, 130
  Nocturnal **216**
  Razor-billed 216, **238–239**
  Sira **218**
  Wattled 216, **218**
Cyanolyca turcosa **28**

Dacnis, Scarlet-breasted **23**
  Tit-like **151**
  Turquoise **23**
Dendrocincla tyrannina **104**
Dendrocygna bicolor **113**
Dendrocygna viduata **232**
Diglossa cyanea **144–145**
Diglossa lafresnayii **120**
Dipper, White-capped **151**
Discosura conversii **29**
Diving-Petrel, Peruvian **71**, **74**
Dotterel, Tawny-throated 161, **165**
Dove, Scaled **127**
  West Peruvian 71, **76**
  White-tipped **50–51**, 244
Duck, Andean **165**
  Black-headed **176**
  Crested **159**, 161

Muscovy **216**
  Torrent **13**

Eagle, Harpy **48**, **216**
Earthcreeper, White-throated **73**
Egret, Snowy **85**, **86**
Egretta thula **85**, **86**
Elaenia, Choco **22**
Embernagra platensis **211**
Emerald, Andean **125**
  Glittering-bellied **244**
Emerald-Toucanet, Southern **105**
Empidonax traillii **258**
Ensifera ensifera **155**, 209
Eriocnemis aline **201**
Eriocnemis luciani **197**
Eriocnemis mosquera **124**
Eubucco bourcierii **23**
Euphonia, Orange-bellied **121**
  Thick-billed **63**, **121**
Euphonia laniirostris **63**
Euphonia xanthogaster **121**
Eurypyga helias **188**

Falcon, Aplomado **161**
  Bat **216**
Field-Tyrant, Short-tailed 58, **74**
Finch, Ash-breasted Sierra **158**
  Black-hooded Sierra **156–157**
  Cochabamba Mountain **148**, **149**, **150**, 151
  Glacier **161**
  Gray-crested **251**
  House **166**
  Peruvian Sierra **156**
  Plumbeous Sierra **166**
  Rufous-sided Warbling **148**
  Slender-billed **73**, **74**
  Tanager 20, **22**
Flamingo, Andean 13, **83**, 161, 162, 165, **176**
  Chilean 74, **82–83**, 161, 162, 165, **176**
  James's 13, 83, **133**, 161, 162, **163**, 165, **176**
Flicker, Andean 52, 161, 165, **175**
Florisuga mellivora **105**
Flowerpiercer, Black **121**
  Glossy **120**
  Masked **144–145**
Fluvicola nengeta **47**
Fluvicola pica **112**
Flycatcher, Acadian **13**
  Alder **57**
  Baird's 54, **58**
  Cinnamon **102**
  Cliff **244**
  Golden-bellied **122**
  Golden-crowned **122**
  Great-crested **258**
  Olive-sided 13, **30**
  Ornate **198**
  Rufous 54, 57, **61**
  Rusty-margined **110**
  Social **110**, **122**

Tawny-breasted **32–33**
  Vermillion **71**
  Willow **258**
Foliage-gleaner, Henna-hooded 54, **58**
Forest-Falcon, Plumbeous **23**
Forpus conspicillatus **121**
Furnarius longirostris **117**

Galbalcyrhynchus purusianus **228**
Geositta peruviana **76**
Geositta punensis **173**
Geospizopsis unicolor **166**
Gnatcatcher, Masked **251**
Gnorimopsar chopi **253**
Golden-Plover, American **161**
Goose, Andean 165, **168**
  Orinoco **230**
Grackle, Carib **107**
  Great-tailed **107**
  Mountain **98**
  Red-bellied **23**, **97**
Grallaria alleni **44**
Grallaria flavotincta **30**
Grallaria gigantea **26**
Grallaria nuchalis **192**
Grallaria ridgelyi **187**
Grallaria ruficapilla **206**
Grallaria saturata **190**
Grallaricula flavirostris **34**
Grebe, Colombian **13**
  Great **74**
  Junin 13, **161**, 162, 165
  Silvery **141**, **161**
  Titicaca 13, **161**, **162**
  White-tufted 74, **173**
Grosbeak, Golden **64**
  Rose-breasted **23**
Ground-Cuckoo, Banded **20**, **23**, **25**, **98**
Ground Dove, Black-winged **138**, **161**
  Golden-spotted **161**
  Picui 244, **254**
  Ruddy **237**
Guan, Andean **100**, 118
  Band-tailed **118**
  Baudo 23, **25**
  White-winged 57, **61**
Guira guira **243**
Gull, Andean 74, **134–135**, 138, 141, 161
  Belcher's 71, **90**
  Franklin's 71, 74, **86**
  Gray **71**, **74**
  Gray-hooded **71**
  Kelp **91**
  Laughing **86**
  Swallow-tailed **71**

Haematopus palliatus **84**, **85**
Hawk, Broad-winged 13, **22**
  Gray-backed 57, **58**
Heliangelus amethysticollis **40–41**
Heliodoxa aurescens **237**
Heliodoxa imperatrix **31**

Heliodoxa jacula **21**
Heliodoxa leadbeateri **183**
Heliodoxa rubinoides **201**
Helmetcrest, Blue-bearded 98, **138**, **139**
  Buffy **139**
Hermit, Tawny-bellied **59**
Heron, Agami **216**
  Capped **239**
  Cocoi **233**
  Zigzag **216**
Hesperoburhinus superciliaris **87**
Hillstar, Andean **161**
  Blue-throated 58, **138**, **139**, **141**, **189**
  Ecuadorian 48, **138**, **139**, **141**
Himantopus mexicanus **93**
Hirundo rustica **258**
Hoatzin 15, **216**, **217**
Honeycreeper, Golden-collared **34**
Hornero, Caribbean **117**
  Pale-legged **117**
  Rufous **244**
Hummingbird, Amazilia 74, **91**
  Giant 13, 132, 141, **161**
  Oasis 71, 74, **91**
  Speckled **56**
  Sword-billed **151**, **155**, 186, 209
  Violet-bellied **46**
  White-bellied **244**
Hypnelus ruficollis **128**

Ibis, Andean **138**, **141**, **161**
  Buff-necked **138**
  Puna 74, 161, **167**
Icterus galbula **258**
Inca, Black **97**
  Collared 64, **180–181**, 185
Inca-Finch, Buff-bridled **61**
  Gray-winged 54, **61**
  Great **75**
Iridophanes pulcherrimus **34**
Ixothraupis rufigula **42**

Jacamar, Purus **228**
  White-eared **228**
  White-throated **223**
Jacana, Wattled **224–225**
Jacana jacana **224–225**
Jacobin, White-necked **105**
Jay, Beautiful **22**
  Turquoise **28**
  White-tailed 54, **58**
Jewelfront, Gould's **237**

Kingbird, Eastern 216, **258**
  Tropical **108**
  Western **108**
Kingfisher, Amazon **104**
  Green **104**
  Green-and-rufous **216**
  Ringed **104**
Kiskadee, Great **110**
Kite, Snail **109**

Lapwing, Andean **161**, **170**
  Southern **170**, **236**
Larosterna inca **70**
Larus belcheri **90**
Leiothlypis peregrina **259**
Leistes militaris **225**
Lepidocolaptes lacrymiger **129**
Leptotila verreauxi **50–51**
Leucocarbo bougainvillii **66–67**
Leucophaeus pipixcan **86**
Loddigesia mirabilis **60**
Lophospingus griseocristatus **251**

Macaw, Blue-and-yellow **212–213**, 216, **235**
  Blue-headed **216**
  Chestnut-fronted **216**
  Great Green 58, **98**
  Green-winged 216, **220–221**
  Red-and-green **212–213**, **234**
  Red-bellied **216**
  Red-fronted **10–11**, 244, 245, 247, **250**, **252**, **257**
  Scarlet 216, **220–221**, **234**
Machetornis rixosa **108**
Manakin, Choco **22**
  Club-winged 20, 22, **189**
  Yellow-headed **23**
Martin, Peruvian 71, 73, **74**
  Purple **244**
Meadowlark, Peruvian **74**
  Red-breasted **225**
  White-browed **225**
Megascops albogularis **204**
Megascops petersoni **199**
Melanerpes cactorum **246**
Metallura tyrianthina **153**
Metaltail, Tyrian **153**
Miner, Coastal 71, 73, 74, **76**
  Common **76**, **173**
  Grayish **74**
  Puna **173**
  Thick-billed 73, **74**
Mitu tuberosum **238–239**
Mniotilta varia **259**
Mockingbird, Floreana **48**
  Long-tailed **74**
Molothrus bonariensis **248**
Momotus momota **219**
Motmot, Amazonian **219**
  Broad-billed **227**
  Rufous **226**
Mountain Tanager, Black-chinned **38**
  Blue-winged 38, **111**
  Golden-backed **186**
  Masked **151**
  Rufous-bellied **148**
  Scarlet-bellied 52, **148**
Mountain-Toucan, Hooded 178, **185**
  Plate-billed **17**, 20, 25
Myiarchus crinitus **258**

Myiobius villosus **32–33**
Myioborus miniatus **194**
Myiodynastes hemichrysus **122**
Myiopsitta monachus **252**
Myiothlypis coronata **117**
Myiotriccus ornatus **198**
Myiozetetes similis **110**

Nannopsittaca dachilleae **230**
Negrito, Andean **161**
Netta peposaca **177**
Nighthawk, Common **216**
  Lesser **54**
  Sand-colored **216**
Nightjar, Scissor-tailed 244, **247**
Numenius phaeopus **82–83**
Nyctibius griseus **116**

Ochthoeca fumicolor **147**
Ocreatus peruanus **198**
Ocreatus underwoodii **22**
Oilbird **189**
Opisthocomus hoazin 15, **217**
Oporornis agilis **259**
Oreotrochilus chimborazo **139**
Oressochen jubatus **230**
Oressochen melanopterus **168**
Oriole, Baltimore **258**
Oropendola, Chestnut-headed **128**
  Crested **128**
Ortalis columbiana **109**
Osprey **74**
Owl, Burrowing 74, **78–79**
Owlet, Long-whiskered **155**, **186**
Oystercatcher, American 71, **84**, **85**
  Blackish **71**, **84**

Palmcreeper, Point-tailed **216**
Pampa-Finch, Great **148**, **211**
Parakeet, Cliff 244, 245, **252**
  Dusky-headed **224–225**, **231**
  El Oro 57, **189**
  Gray-cheeked 54, **58**
  Green-cheeked 244, **247**
  Mitred 244, **248**
  Monk 244, 245, **252**
  Mountain **75**
  Red-masked **248**
  Rufous-fronted **139**
  Scarlet-fronted **248**
  Sinú **13**
  White-eyed **248**
  White-winged **254**
  Yellow-chevroned 244, 247, **254**
Parkesia noveboracensis **258**
Parrot, Blue-headed **224–225**, 225
  Mealy **224–225**
  Orange-cheeked **224–225**
  Red-billed **200**
  Rose-faced **36**
  Scaly-naped **200**
  Turquoise-fronted 244, **250**
  Yellow-eared 97, 98, **130**

Parrotlet, Amazonian 230
   Cobalt-rumped 230
   Dusky-billed 230
   Spectacled 121
   Yellow-faced 54, 57, 61
Pelecanus thagus 87
Pelican, Brown 87
   Peruvian 71, 74, 87
Penelope argyrotis 118
Penelope montagnii 100
Penguin, Humboldt 73, 74, 92–93
   Magellanic 92
Petrel, Cape 74
   Cook's 73
Pewee, Smoke-colored 30
   Tumbes 58
Phaethornis syrmatophorus 59
Phalarope, Red-necked 71
   Wilson's 161, 165
Phalcoboenus carunculatus 140, 141
Pharomachrus fulgidus 102
Pheucticus chrysogaster 64
Pheucticus ludovicianus 259
Phleocryptes melanops 80
Phoenicoparrus andinus 176
Phoenicoparrus jamesi 133, 163
Phoenicopterus chilensis 82–83
Phrygilus atriceps 156–157
Phytotoma rutila 244
Piaya cayana 122
Piculet, Speckle-chested 61
Piha, Chestnut-capped 20, 98
Pilherodius pileatus 239
Pintail, White-cheeked 77
   Yellow-billed 142, 159, 161
Pionus menstruus 224–225, 225
Pipit, Correndera 161
   Yellowish 233
Piranga olivacea 259
Piranga rubra 27, 259
Plantcutter, Peruvian 54, 57, 61
   White-tipped 244
Plegadis ridgwayi 167
Plover, Puna 161, 176
   Snowy 74, 176
Plushcap 151
Pochard, Rosy-billed 177
Poecilotriccus luluae 54–55
Poikilocarbo gaimardi 81
Polioptila dumicola 251
Poorwill, Choco 22
Poospiza garleppi 150
Poospizopsis hypochondria 148
Potoo, Common 116
Protonotaria citrea 259
Psarocolius wagleri 128
Pseudasthenes cactorum 72
Pseudocolaptes johnsoni 27
Psittacara mitratus 248
Pteroglossus torquatus 43, 49
Puffbird, Chestnut-capped 222
   Russet-throated 128
   Spot-backed 244

Swallow-winged 216
Puffleg, Black-breasted 25, 139
   Colorful 23
   Emerald-bellied 186, 201
   Golden-breasted 124
   Gorgeted 98
   Hoary 22
   Sapphire-vented 197
   Turquoise-throated 13, 23
Pygmy-Owl, Ferruginous 247
Pyrilia barrabandi 224–225
Pyrilia pulchra 36
Pyrrhomyias cinnamomeus 102

Quetzal, Crested 102
   White-tipped 102
Quiscalus lugubris 107

Racket-tail, Peruvian 22, 198
   Rufous-booted 198
   White-booted 22, 198
Rail, Black 73, 161
   Bogotá 97
   Junín 162
   Plumbeous 74, 161
Ramphocelus flammigerus 40
Ramphocelus nigrogularis 229
Recurvirostra andina 160
Redstart, American 259
   Slate-throated 194
Rhea, Greater 165
   Lesser/Puna 158, 164, 165
Rhea pennata 164
Rhodopis vesper 91
Rollandia rolland 173
Rostrhamus sociabilis 109
Rupicola peruvianus 95
Rushbird, Wren-like 71, 80, 161

Sabrewing, Gray-breasted 197
   Santa Marta 98
Sandpiper, Baird's 48, 61, 71, 161
   Buff-breasted 48, 216
   Pectoral 161, 216
   Solitary 258
   Stilt 71
Sandpiper-Plover, Diademed 75, 161, 165
Sapphire, Golden-tailed 196
Sapphirewing, Great 25
Schiffornis, Varzea 216
Screamer, Horned 58
Screech-Owl, Choco 22
   Cinnamon 186, 199
   White-throated 204
Seedeater, Drab 73
   Variable 46
Seed-Finch, Large-billed 58
Seedsnipe, Gray-breasted 161, 168
   Least 71, 74, 168
   Rufous-bellied 13, 138, 141, 161, 165, 168
Setophaga castanea 259

Setophaga fusca 203, 259
Setophaga ruticilla 259
Setophaga striata 259
Sheartail, Peruvian 71, 75, 91
Shearwater, Buller's 73
   Sooty 74
Shiffornis, Varzea 216
Sirystes, Choco 22
Siskin, Black 148, 161
   Hooded 169
   Olivaceous 169
   Red 98
   Saffron 169
   Thick-billed 148, 169
Snipe, Imperial 25
   Puna 161
Solitaire, Black 20
Sparrow, Black-striped 123
   Olive 114
   Orange-billed 210
   Rufous-collared 174, 244
Spatula cyanoptera 88
Spatula puna 159
Spatuletail, Marvelous 13, 60, 61, 186
Spheniscus humboldti 92–93
Spinetail, Blackish-headed 54, 57, 58
   Great 54
   Marañon 57
Spinus magellanicus 169
Sporathraupis cyanocephala 193
Sporophila corvina 46
Starfrontlet, Buff-winged 97
   Dusky 97, 139
Starthroat, Blue-tufted 244, 247
Stilpnia cyanicollis 208
Stilpnia heinei 129
Stilpnia vitriolina 99
Stilt, Black-necked 93
Stork, Jabiru 216
Storm-Petrel, Markham's 71, 74
   Ringed 71, 74
   White-vented 74
Sula variegata 88–89
Sunangel, Gorgeted 22, 40–41
   Royal 155, 178, 182, 186
   Purple-backed 57
   Shining 25, 136, 151
Sunbeam, Black-hooded 185
Sunbittern 188, 189
Sungrebe 216
Surfbird 69, 74
Swallow, Barn 258
   Tumbes 61
Swift, Andean 244
   Chimney 73
Sylph, Long-tailed 44, 205
   Violet-tailed 22, 45, 205

Tachuris rubrigasta 80
Tachyphonus rufus 60
Tanager, Beryl-spangled 129
   Black-and-gold 23

   Black-bellied 229
   Black-capped 129
   Blue-capped 193
   Blue-gray 179, 185, 254
   Blue-necked 208
   Buff-bellied 54, 61
   Flame-faced 35
   Flame-rumped 40
   Glaucous 178
   Glistening-green 31
   Golden 18–19
   Golden-naped 126–127
   Gold-ringed 20, 23, 24, 25, 97
   Guira 216
   Inti 242
   Magpie 185
   Masked Crimson 229
   Moss-backed 20, 24, 25
   Multicolored 97
   Ochre-breasted 36
   Palm 185, 228
   Paradise 189, 208
   Rufous-throated 42
   Sayaca 178, 244, 255
   Scarlet 216, 259
   Scrub 99
   Silver-beaked 229
   Summer 13, 22, 27, 259
   Swallow 189, 216
   White-capped 28
   White-lined 60
   Yellow-green 23
   Yellow-scarfed 186
Tangara arthus 18–19
Tangara parzudakii 35
Tapaculo, Choco 22
   Ecuadorian 57
   Ocellated 22
   Vilcabamba 148
Teal, Blue-winged 88
   Brazilian 214
   Cinnamon 74, 77, 88
   Puna 159, 161
   Yellow-billed 143, 170
Tern, Elegant 74, 75
   Inca 70, 71, 74
   Large-billed 216
   Peruvian 73, 74
   Royal 74, 75, 77
Thalasseus elegans 75
Thalasseus maximus 75, 77
Thalurania colombica 47, 101
Thalurania furcata 191
Thamnophilus doliatus 124
Thamnophilus unicolor 53
Theristicus branickii 138
Thick-knee, Peruvian 71, 74, 87
Thinocorus orbignyianus 168
Thornbill, Olivaceous 148
   Rainbow-bearded 138
Thornbird, Chestnut-backed 54, 61
Thorntail, Green 29
Thraupis episcopus 179

Thraupis palmarum 228
Thraupis sayaca 255
Thripadectes holostictus 108
Thrush, Black-billed 119
   Chiguanco 166
   Creamy-bellied 244, 249
   Gray-cheeked 258
   Great 166, 185
   Marañon 61
   Swainson's 13, 22, 34, 57, 185, 199, 202, 244, 258
Tiger-Heron, Fasciated 54
Tinamotis pentlandii 171
Tinamou, Choco 22
   Gray 189
   Little 106
   Puna 158, 161, 165, 171
   Taczanowski's 161, 162
Tit-Spinetail, Andean 141
   Streaked 73
   White-browed 148, 149
Tit-Tyrant, Ash-breasted 148, 149
   Pied-crested 73
Tody-Flycatcher, Johnson's 54–55, 183, 186
Toucan, Choco 20, 22
Toucanet, Crimson-rumped 39
Treehunter, Striped 108
Treerunner, Pearled 185
Tringa flavipes 258
Tringa melanoleuca 79
Tringa solitaria 258
Trogon, Choco Black-throated 22
   Collared 196, 200
   Masked 196, 200
Trogon collaris 200
Trogon personatus 196
Tuftedcheek, Buffy 27
   Pacific 27
   Streaked 52, 185
Turdus amaurochalinus 249
Turdus fuscater 166
Turdus ignobilis 119
Tyrannulet, Choco 22
   Tumbes 58
Tyrannus tyrannus 258
Tyrant, Cattle 108, 127
   Many-colored Rush 71, 80, 161
   Tumbes 58
   White-headed Marsh 112

Umbrellabird, Long-wattled 20, 22, 23, 189
Uranomitra franciae 125
Urosticte benjamini 42

Vanellus chilensis 236
Vanellus resplendens 170
Violetear, Brown 107
   Lesser 62, 202
   Sparkling 62, 202
Vireo, Choco 22, 25
   Red-eyed 258
Vireo olivaceus 258

Vulture, Black 227
   King 54, 61, 216
   Turkey 227

Wagtail-Tyrant, Greater 244
Warbler, Bay-breasted 259
   Black-and-white 259
   Blackburnian 13, 22, 185, 203, 259
   Blackpoll 216, 259
   Buff-rumped 32
   Canada 13, 22, 25, 259
   Cerulean 13, 48
   Choco 22
   Connecticut 259
   Prothonotary 259
   Russet-crowned 117
   Canada 48
   Tennesssee 259
Warbling-Finch, Ringed 244, 245
Waterthrush, Northern 258
Water-Tyrant, Masked 47
   Pied 112
Whimbrel 71, 74, 82–83
Whistling-Duck, Fulvous 113, 232
   White-faced 113, 232
Whitetip, Purple-bibbed 42
Woodcreeper, Long-billed 216
   Montane 129
   Narrow-billed 244
   Strong-billed 207
   Tyrannine 104
Woodnymph, Crowned 47, 101, 191
   Fork-tailed 191
Woodpecker, Black-necked 71, 75
   Choco 22
   Crimson-crested 191
   Scarlet-backed 54, 58
   White-fronted 244, 246, 247
Wood-Pewee, Eastern 30, 258
   Western 244
Wood-Quail, Dark-backed 23, 25
Woodstar, Chilean 73
   Esmeraldas 57
   White-bellied 65
Wood-Wren, Bar-winged 155, 182, 186
   Gray-breasted 185
   Munchique 23
Wren, Apolinar's 98
   Fasciated 58
   Inca 151
   Superciliated 54, 58

Xiphocolaptes promeropirhynchus 207

Yellow-Finch, Grassland 71
   Puna 161
   Raimondi's 73
Yellowlegs, Greater 79
   Lesser 79, 161, 258

Zenaida meloda 76
Zonotrichia capensis 174